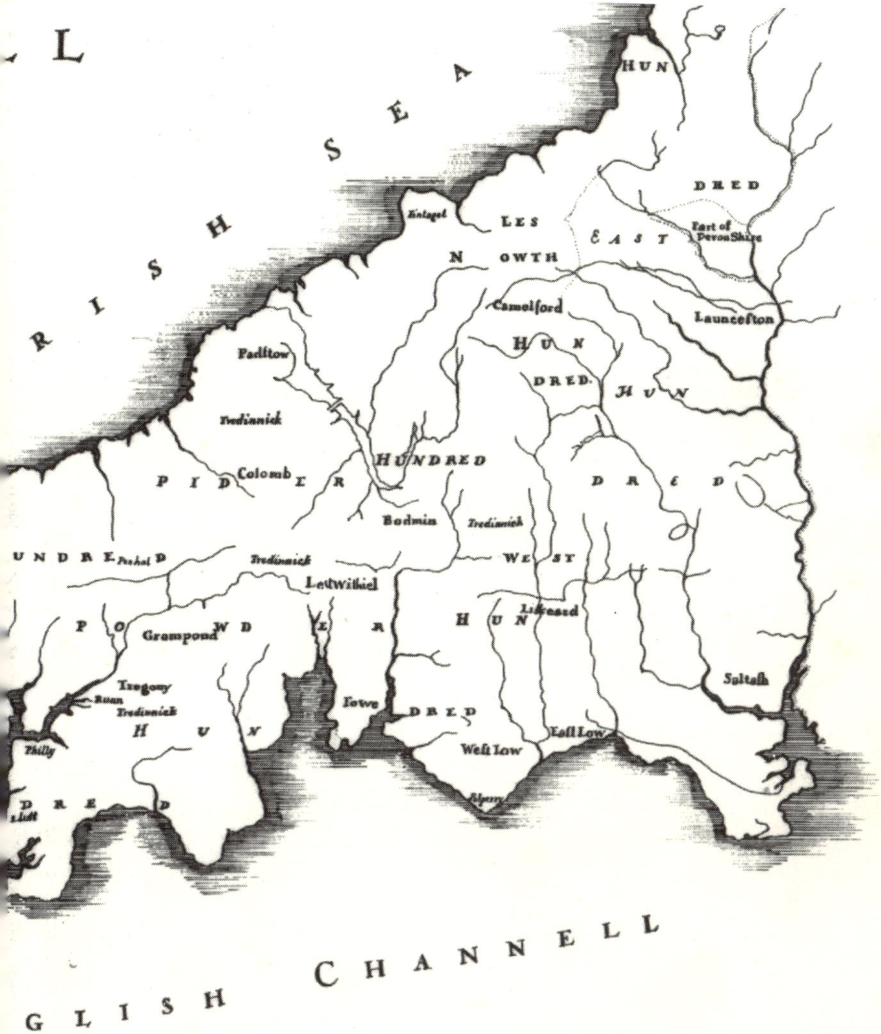
L
RISH SEA
HUN
DRED
East of Devon Shire
EAST
Kintagel
LES
NOWTH
Camelford
Launceston
HUN
DRED.
HUN
Padstow
Tredinnick
HUNDRED
Colomb
PID ER
DRED
Bodmin
Tredinnick
UNDRE D
Tredinnick
WEST
Lestwithiel
Liskeard
HUN
POWDER
Grampound
Saltash
Tregony
Ruan
Tredinnick
Fowe
DRED
HUN
East Low
West Low
Philly
DRED
GLISH CHANNELL

'A Taste of Cornwall'

RECIPES AND RAMBLINGS

Edited by Ann Butcher
and
Kenneth Fraser Annand

WITH
ARTICLES BY KENNETH FRASER ANNAND

Tredinnick Press

'A TASTE OF CORNWALL'
(Series)

RECIPES AND RAMBLINGS

© TREDINNICK PRESS 1994
Published by Tredinnick Press,
Burnwithian House, St. Day, Cornwall.

ISBN 0 9523407 1 2

A.B. dedicates this book to her Father,
Ronald Burns Butcher.
K. F A. dedicates this book to his Mother,
Marjorie Fraser Annand.

This book is sold subject to the condition that it shall not, by way of trade or otherwise, be lent, resold, hired out, or otherwise circulated without the publisher's prior consent in any form of binding or cover other than that in which it is published and without a similar condition including this condition being imposed on the subsequent purchaser.

All rights reserved. This publication either in whole or in part may not be reproduced, stored in a retrieval system or transmitted in any form or by any means, electronic, mechanical, photographic, or otherwise, without prior permission in writing of the copyright holders.

Film origination by: Xpress Repro of Truro.
Printed by: Hartnolls of Bodmin.
Typeset in Perpetua on Apple Macintosh

Front and back cover photographs by:
Howard Speirs Esq[re] of Perranporth, Cornwall.

Photograph opposite: Dawn at Carn Brea Castle.

By Tre, Pol and Pen,
You may know the Cornishmen.

There's pasties and Cream,
Tin in the stream,
Pilchards and Herrings
They sparkle and gleam.
Though we may roam
Cornwall's our home,
The beautiful County of Cornwall!

Soup

Augustus was a chubby lad;
Fat ruddy cheeks Augustus had;
And every body saw with joy
The plump and hearty healthy boy.
He ate and drank as he was told,
And never let his soup get cold.
But one day, one cold winter's day,
He scream'd out – "Take the soup away!
O take the nasty soup away!
I won't have any soup today."

Next day, now look, the picture shows
How lank and lean Augustus grows!
Yet, though he feels so weak and ill,
The naughty fellow cries out still –
"Not any soup for me, I say:
O take the nasty soup away!
I won't have any soup today."

The third day comes; Oh what a sin!
To make himself so pale and thin.
Yet, when the soup is put on table,
He screams, as loud as he is able, –
"Not any soup for me, I say:
O take the nasty soup away!
I won't have any soup today."

Look at him, now the fourth day's come!
He scarcely weighs a sugar-plum;
He's like a little bit of thread,
and on the fifth day, he was – dead!

Dr. Heinrich Hoffmann.
(Taken from 'The English Struwwelpeter').

Treviskey Soup
(An Adaptable Feast)

Take the bones and any bits of meat left from a cooked Chicken, Turkey, Goose, Pheasant et cetera. Cover with water in a large saucepan and add Salt, Pepper and a quartered Onion. Bring to the boil, then simmer for 3 - 4 hours. Let it stand overnight and next day repeat the simmering, topping up with liquid as it evaporates. When cool, strain into a clean saucepan.

From now on, YOU decide its thickness and taste. Taste frequently and add a little of that which you think would blend into a good soup.

Suggestions:
Start with a teaspoon or two of one or more of the following: Marmite; Tomato Purée; added Salt and Pepper; Marjoram; ground Ginger; Worcester Sauce; perhaps a little Nutmeg and certainly some Brown Sugar. Taste and blend as you go at each addition. Orange Juice or tinned Peaches - puréed, make a delicious addition too; sometimes a little puréed Chutney works wonders. You will soon find out those which you like and the combinations that work.

Now start thickening with Fine Oatmeal. Allow a handful to trickle into the pan slowly, while you stir until it is smoothly incorporated. Repeat until thickening starts, then let it all simmer as long as possible - 2 to 3 hours at least, watching and adding a little Milk as the liquid evaporates, or a little more Oatmeal to make a good thick soup. Finally, when ready, you can add a wine glass of Port or Sherry. Serve with a tablespoon of thick Cream on each bowlful of soup.

There are endless possibilities, but when you taste, savour each spoonful and decide what you would like to add. With a bit of practice, I assure you that your soup will be in great demand.

Mrs. Fraser Annand,
Treviskey.

PARSNIP AND ASPARAGUS SOUP
(FROM THE ROSELAND INN, PHILLEIGH)

1lb. Parsnips (peeled)
½ lb. Asparagus
1 oz. Butter
2 tablespoons Single Cream

4 tablespoons Natural Yoghurt
4 Egg Yolks
Salt and Pepper to taste

Prepare parsnips and asparagus. Cook in salted water until tender. Drain asparagus and cut off the tips, keeping these separately until the end of the recipe. Melt butter in about 2 pints of cooking liquid. Blend the vegetables until puréed with the liquid and return all to the saucepan. Stir in the cream and yoghurt and heat gently for 5 minutes. Whisk eggs in a bowl with a little of the soup and then incorporate. Do not allow the soup to boil. A few minutes before serving, add the asparagus tips. With a circular motion, dribble into the tureen or bowls a little single cream to garnish.

[Editor: I am most grateful to Jacqui and Graham Hill; for this warming and delicious recipe, which I recommend and for the delightful photograph of the Roseland Inn under snow - a very rare occurrence for usually, in the words of the late Mr Edward Harte - who will be remembered by many - "there is no real winter in Roseland".]

Mrs. Hill, Roseland Inn, Philleigh-in-Roseland.

SARAH'S MUSHROOM SAVOURY

White Sauce
Mushrooms
Onions
St. Austell Bay Shrimps

Clotted Cream
Brandy
Salt
Black Pepper

Fry together the mushrooms and onions. Make a white sauce by the roux method. Add mushrooms; onions; shrimps; clotted cream; salt and pepper to taste and brandy before serving.

Mrs. Peter Wilkinson,
(alias Lily Champney.)

Roseland Inn, at Philleigh-in-Roseland.

Dame Nellie's Paté

1 lb. Pigs liver
½ lb. Belly Pork
¼ lb. home-cured
    Streaky Bacon
1 large Onion (fried first)
2 tablespoons Tomato purée
3 Cloves of Garlic
¼ pint Red Wine

Brandy
Grated Lemon Rind
Basil and Herbs to taste
2 Bay Leaves
Black Pepper
Pinch of Salt
Cornish Clotted Cream

1   Chop meat and put into fireproof dish.
2   Add fried onion and all other ingredients, placing Bay Leaves on top.
3   Cook in range for 1 - 1½ hours.
4   Remove Bay Leaves and put the partly cooked paté through a coarse mincing machine (a modern blender serves very well).
5   Firm down meat into paté dish, replacing the Bay Leaves.
6   Steam in a Bain-Marie for approximately 1 further hour.
7   Press well and leave to go cold.

[This Recipe was given to the Editor by Dame Nellie's daughter.   Cornwall was her favoured place for holidays.]

Chonion Tart

(Wartime recipe - Second World War)

Short Pastry made with:
6 ozs. Plain Flour
3½ ozs. fat (lard or mixture of lard and butter)

Chopped cooked Onion
Grated Cheese

Line tartlet tins with pastry, chop and gently cook onions until just soft. Place a little grated cheese in the bottom of each pastry case, followed by layers of onion and grated cheese alternately, topping with grated cheese. Bake in moderate oven for about 20 minutes until nicely browned.

"These were christened Chonion Tarts by my brother when on leave. He was chief engineer on a Motor Torpedo Boat".

Cornish Vegetable Soup with Hog's Pudding

1 Swede
2 Parsnips
2 Carrots
1 Onion
2 Celery sticks

¼ lb. Red Lentils
2 potatoes
4 pints of stock and herbs
Hog's Pudding

Chop the vegetables finely and soften in a little vegetable oil. Add the herbs and plenty of salt and pepper. Pour on the stock, add the lentils, bring to the boil then simmer for an hour. Lightly mash the soup so that there are still some chunks of vegetable left.

Before serving remove the skin from the Hog's pudding, slice into ½" rounds and fry lightly. Place a few in each soup bowl and pour the soup over the top. Chop some parsley finely and scatter liberally, then add a spoonful of Clotted Cream if required.

Ann Butcher, St. Day.

Stilton Soup from Gwennap

2 ozs. Butter
1 Onion - finely chopped
2 Celery sticks - sliced
1½ ozs. Flour
3 tablespoons Dry White Wine
1½ pints Stock (poultry or feathered game)
½ pint Milk

4 ozs. Stilton - crumbled (and well ripe)
2 ozs. Cheddar - grated
4 tablespoons Clotted Cream
Mace - to taste
Lemon Juice - to taste
Salt - to taste
Black Pepper - to taste

Melt butter in a saucepan, add the vegetables and fry gently for 5 minutes. Stir in the flour and cook for a further minute. Remove from heat and stir in the wine and the stock. Return to the heat, bring to the boil and simmer for 30 minutes. Add the milk and cheese, stirring constantly. Season to taste and stir in the clotted cream. Put through a sieve (or purée in a blender). Reheat without boiling.

N.B. If the Stilton is not sufficiently ripe, you will require more than the 4 ozs. in the recipe.
This quantity serves between 4 and 6 persons.

K. F A.

Fish, Foods, Famines and Fables

"*The Vicar of St. Ives says the smell of fish there is sometimes so terrific as to stop the Church clock*", so wrote the Revd. Francis Kilvert on the 21st. July 1870.

Did the Vicar of St. Ives consider this an important sign or portend? The ancient Greek word for fish is ΙΧΘΥΣ (pronounced Ichthys) and this word was taken up as a secret sign by the early persecuted Christians. It probably stems from the miracle of the loaves and fishes and other references to fish used by our Lord, for example - 'I shall make you fishers of men'. Indeed the mnemonics of the Greek spelling are used by the Christian Church to stand for 'Jesus Christ God's Son Saviour'. The secret sign of the fish appears in the catacombs in Rome and it may have been used as a sign of safety by the early Christian when meeting someone not previously known to him. The Christian may have marked half the sign in the sand with his foot or stick and then waited to see if the other half was reciprocated by his new acquaintance.

Perhaps the stopping of the Church clock was a sign to the fishermen of St. Ives to divide their time more evenly between material gain and spiritual gain. So why the link between fish and time? To the believer, man's time is surely as nought in the greater span and one is constantly reminded in this 'naughty world' that 'God's time is best'. Bach used this as the title to his Lutheran

Church Cantata No. 106 - 'Gottes Zeit ist die allerbeste Zeit'. It is a mourning cantata, possibly having been written for a funeral service in 1707, when certainly man's time would have stopped for the gentleman concerned. It is actually the most profoundly radiant work, but I digress, for Kilvert does not enlighten us with regard to the Vicar of St. Ives's musical taste, or his musings as to the hidden meaning behind the demise of the Church clock. It is possible that a less esoteric explanation might revolve round the old saying - 'all hands on deck', for the landing of a full seine of pilchards in those days would most certainly have involved work for the greater majority of the community. It is an astonishing fact that in 1851, the largest ever recorded catch of pilchards produced 5,600 hogsheads, the winder had neglected his duties because he was far too busy with his catch. It seems that the clock did stop at the smelliest moments!

The smell of fish has been a dominant feature in the lives of the Cornish since time began and certainly before the fishermen of St. Ives depended upon the vagaries of their Church clock. Undoubtedly, the industry has seen vast changes during this century, not only in the methods employed but also with regard to the type of fish caught which have variously included: pilchards; bream; hake; pollock; conger eel; herring; turbot; mackerel; skate; ray; cod; ling - particularly off the Isles of Scilly; whiting; shrimps; cockles; mussels and limpets. Dogfish was often made into broth known as Morgay Soup, from the Cornish 'môr' meaning sea and 'ki' meaning dog - indeed is this the origin of the word 'seadog'? Lance (or sand eels) were twitched out of the sand by iron crooks on moonlight nights and for the grander tables of the gentry, lobster; crabs and crayfish were served - thought to be far 'too good' for the poor people, who occasionally added seal to their menus.

Since ancient times, there have always been oyster beds in the creeks off the south coast and in particular those of the Helford River, Restronguet, Percuil and others leading into the Carrick Roads. Certain of these oyster beds have been the cause of concern over recent months since the closure of Wheal Jane tin mine in 1991, when pumping operations ceased. To quote from the National Rivers Authority South Western Region publication 'Wheal Jane - A Clear

Women buying fish at Newlyn - about 1900.

Way Forward' - 'As the water level in the mine began to rise and in anticipation of a heavily contaminated discharge of mine water polluting the Carnon River, the NRA instigated a temporary treatment system. Mine water reached the surface in November 1991, but events then took a turn for the worse.' 'Over 10 million gallons of heavily contaminated water burst from the disused Cornish tin mine workings of Wheal Jane, causing serious pollution.' 'The dramatic burst arose when a plug in the underground Nangiles Adit unexpectedly failed in January 1992.' Since February 1992 there has existed a complicated system for temporary treatment including Lime Dosing - to neutralise acidity; a tailings dam and polishing lagoon. Between February 1992 and February 1994 these measures have prevented 900 tonnes of heavy metals from being deposited in the estuary. The NRA is now examining various methods for long-term treatment which include an Anoxic pond; an Anoxic Limestone drain; an Acrobic Cell with water filled reed beds; an anaerobic cell and rock filters. The problem is very much under control and seems to have caused no long term effects to marine life.

But for all this abundance from the sea, there was often a 'catch' of a different nature. The Eighteenth Century brought famines to Cornwall culminating in the most disastrous one in 1794 - 1795 which was caused by the tremendous scarcity of corn and the greed of the corn merchants, whose milling charges were outrageously high. An additional factor was the millers' desire to secure for themselves greater prices by sending the little corn they did have, out of the County. The general populace of Cornwall were literally starving. Regular rioting occurred throughout the whole County and attempts were even made, by the great and the good, (who fully believed the peasants <u>were</u> revolting!) to obtain imported cargoes of grain, paid for by public subscription. The populace survived on fish, if they could afford to buy it and the starving coastal dweller gathered limpets and other shellfish. To the ubiquitous broth, which had always been the staple diet of the Cornishman into which every scrap imaginable went with alacrity, was also often added snails. The Cornish Gazette for the 4th April 1801 reported with regard to the riots: 'Whilst scarcely a town in the County has escaped the contagion, in the markets it had been chiefly confined to the lower order of women only. *[Editor: I quote history - no poison-pen letters, please!]* In the mining districts, however, large bodies of tinners have assembled, particularly in the neighbourhood of St. Austell, where they went round to the farmers, carrying a written paper in one hand and a rope in the other. If the farmers hesitated to sign the paper, which pledged them to sell their corn at a reduced price, the rope was fastened about their necks and they were terrified into compliance.' This also occurred in St. Ives and other places.

Pilchards were the main diet and in 1812 the landings of fish were particularly large, but because of lack of sales the farmers were using them to manure the land. An incredible thought when the population was still experiencing vast shortages of all food. The problem appears to have been due directly to a salt tax and the Revd. Mr. Warren (in his 'Tour through Cornwall' of 1809) states that: 'Each cottager on an average is wont to lay in about a thousand fish for winter use. The quantity of salt necessary is about seven pounds to one hundredweight of fish. Until the late rise in the duty of that article salt might be procured at 1½d. per pound and the whole stock cured at an expense of 8s.9d. But tempora mutantur; salt is now increased to 4d. per pound and a thousand fish cannot be cured under £1.3s. 4d., a sum of unobtainable magnitude to a poor man who gets only 6s. or, at most 7s. per week for his labours.' A.K. Hamilton Jenkin, to whom I am indebted for some of my factual research, in his excellent book 'Cornwall and its People' tells us that the Bishop of Exeter intervened in the plight of the populace of the Isles of Scilly, and via the Lords of the Treasury, quantities of salt were sent to the Islanders for salting their fish to prevent actual starvation during the following winter.

All manner of fish was salted and cured in a bussa[1] and the most popular - cured pilchards, were known as 'fumadoe' or 'fair maids'. Pilchards were also scrowled (grilled) and were often known as 'scrowlers'. The oil from pilchards was utilized in a 'chyl' or 'chylla' for lighting cottage homes.

Of course, as always, there were those who fared better - maids or no; for instance the cottager with his goat and the farmer of the moorland sheep. With the more fertile areas of the south coast, the

---

(1) bussa* = *coarse earthenware vessel with or without a lid in many different sizes. Some had two carrying handles.*
**See pictures of ancient cooking equipment at Helston Folk Museum - page 114.*

dairy cow was making its mark by the Eighteenth Century.

As I have mentioned, seals sometimes joined the menu and in 1825 Robert Stephen Hawker (1813-1875), the famous Victorian eccentric, author and Vicar of Morwenstow travelled with a friend to Boscastle. Hawker was an interesting man and as Piers Brendon informs us in his book, 'Hawker of Morwenstow', that unusual cleric talked to birds and used to invite his nine cats into Church with him. He proceeded to excommunicate one of them for catching a mouse on the Sabbath. History does not relate those which were his feelings upon discovering the truth about a meal of which he and his friend partook at the Ship Inn in Boscastle, kept at that time by a certain Joan Treworgy. Hamilton Jenkin tells the story: ' "What had she got in the house?" they asked. "Meat" replied the landlady, "meat and taties". The specific difference between beef, mutton, veal etc., seemed to be utterly or artfully ignored; and to every frenzied enquiry her calm, inexorable reply was: "Meat - nice wholesome meat and taties".'

'In due time', continues Hawker, 'we sat down to a not unsatisfactory meal, but it is a wretched truth that by no effort could we ascertain what it was that was roasted for us that day by Widow Treworgy and which we consumed. "Was it a piece of Boscastle baby?" I suggested to my companion. The question caused him to rush out and enquire; but he came back baffled and shouting: "Meat and taties". There was not a vestige of bone, nor any outline that could identify the joint and the not unsavoury taste was something like tender veal. It was not until years afterwards that light was thrown on our mysterious dinner that day by a passage which I accidentally turned up in an ancient history of Cornwall. Therein I read 'that the people of Bouscastle and Boussiney do catch in the summer seas divers young soyles (seals) which, doubtful if they be fish or flesh, conynge housewives will nevertheless roast and do make thereof savoury meat'.'

The labouring classes and in particular the miners existed largely on potatoes and turnips or leeks which they constructed into the well known pasty and if they were lucky this might include a little meat.

Mr. Hamilton Jenkin tells us 'the Cornish miner liked a diet which would 'stand up' to his surroundings' and quotes a story to prove his point of 'a certain man who married a cook who had formerly been in the service of a wealthy family. On going to the mine one day shortly afterwards he took with him a pasty of his wife's making. "How did you like your pasty?" was the question asked on his return - "Aw 'a wadn' no good at all" came the disappointing reply "time I got down fifty fathoms 'a were scat to lembs' (broken to fragments). The wans mawther made wadn' break if they'd a faaled to the bottom of the shaft. They <u>was</u> paasties, you!".'

The Miner's pasty had to be built for endurance. On occasions they were heated on the steam boilers of the mine by their wives who were working as bal-maidens[1] (these women broke up the ore with club hammers). They then literally dropped them down the shaft to their husbands below. The miners pasty was also often double ended, meat and vegetables one end and fruit at the other - often blackberries when in season.

The Cornish pasty or Tiddly Oggie can and is made out of anything going and has been the staple diet of the County from time immemorial. The pasty was often marked with a prospective owner's initial to show which contained his preferred filling. It has long been upheld that the Devil never crossed the Tamar into Cornwall, either because he was not sufficiently courageous to sample the contents of a Cornishwoman's pasty, or because he was afraid of ending up in one! Indeed the various round houses in the County, the most famous of which are at Veryan, were supposed to have been built in that manner in order to provide no corners in which the Devil could hide - presumably as an insurance policy for the 'doubting Thomas'. The pasty came in many different guises depending upon the preferred filling which might be: meat and potato; mackerel; apple; apple 'n hinge (the pluck, lungs and heart of an animal); broccoli; chicken; date; eggy; herby; jam; parsley; pork; rabbity; rice; turnip and not forgetting the star-gazing pasty - in this one the herring or mackerel head sticks out of one end and its tail protrudes from the other and it

---

(1) Bal-maidens = bal or wheal means mine.
(2) fringle fire = kitchen fire.
(3) crock* = a three legged iron pot or kettle.
(4) brandis* = a three legged iron trivet to support a saucepan over the fire or an open hearth.
(5) furzy tobs = the cut tops of furze or gorse generally used for cooking fuel and for heating the clome oven.

*See pictures of ancient cooking equipment at Helston Folk Museum - page 114.

is stuffed with the same stuffing 'yow do have in mabiers' (chickens). 'That' we are told 'was some nice pasty too, cooked in a fringle[2] fire with crock[3] and brandis[4] and old furzy tobs[5]". From the stargazing pasty, it is but a brief step to the star-gazy pie - same sort of thing, but this time the most common ingredients were seven or eight pilchards with the heads poking out through the centre of the pastry crust. Pies, too, came in all forms including: apple and spice; apple and mutton; eel; conger; duck; curlew; goose giblet; herby; likky (leek); mince; muggity (sheep's pluck); parsley; rook and squab (young pigeon) to name but a few.

Having feasted upon these delicacies and slept the sleep of the just, or just not sober if one had accompanied the feasting with mahogany or shenagrum (another story), there was breakfast to which one could look forward not, I imagine, with unbounded joy and enthusiasm. How about starting your day staring into the watery eyes of the disgustingly ugly sisters: Gerty Grey and Gerty Milk? The former was a creation containing seasoned flour and water eaten hot, but kept thin. The latter, obviously a great improvement for the 'well to do' peasant, contained flour and milk, seasoned, eaten hot and kept runny. As to the state of one's constitution and stomach in particular - I leave the reader to conjecture!

Fishwives at Newlyn - about 1890.

Gurnard or Gurnet
(Stuffed and Baked)

Cut off the head and trim off the dorsal fin and other fins. Press down firmly on the backbone to release flesh from spine. Slice the fish down the backbone from the underside upward. Remove skeleton and other bones. Fill with desired stuffing. Grease casserole dish and a piece of greaseproof paper. Parcel up the fish in the greaseproof paper and bake in a moderate oven. Serve with Asparagus Sauce. (See under 'Sauces'.)

Mackerel

Mackerel is delicious stuffed with Creamed Chestnut and Brandy Stuffing (see under 'Stuffings') and served with either Anchovy Sauce; Gooseberry Sauce or Horseradish Sauce. (See under 'Sauces'.)

Salmon Cutlets

This is a delicious entrée. Take half a salmon cutlet for each person and poach lightly. Serve with Lemon and Cream Sauce (see under 'Sauces'). Garnish with a sprig of Basil and rounds of Lemon.

Salting Pilchards and Mackerel

Take a Bussa or earthenware Salter (bath shaped, with handles). *[Editor: See picture of old Cornish cooking equipment within this book.]* Clean and gut the fish and fill the insides with salt. Place the fish in layers and sprinkle more salt over the fish. Cover with cloth or lid.

Limpets

Only collect limpets from places that are washed by the salt tide and not anywhere near habitation. Remove from the rocks with a sharp blow or by a knife. Clean off sand and place in a pan of cold water.

Bring to the boil and continue to cook until they slip from their shells. Serve with a vinaigrette including ground black pepper and a little mustard, olive oil, white wine vinegar and lemon juice.

To 'Scrowl' Pilchards

Clean and gut fish. Cut open and season with salt, black pepper and a little sugar. Leave for a few hours and 'scrowl' between a gridiron over a bright fire.

Mussels

Gather from the cleanest places and nowhere near human dwellings or sewage outfalls. Place them in fresh water for some hours. Change the water frequently. It is essential that all shellfish is alive and healthy before cooking and eating. Discard mussels with slightly open or gaping shells, or any that do not close when tapped. With a stiff brush, thoroughly scrub and clean the shells under the cold tap. Scrape away the black weed, or beard, from the outside of the shells. Shells open during cooking. Place in a heavy based pan with half an inch of water or white wine and chopped parsley and shallots or onions. Cook with the lid on for about five minutes over a low heat until the shells open. If they do not open, you may assume the fish 'have been gathered and rejoice with us but upon another shore.' Discard them!

Cockles

Dig them out and leave in fresh water through the night. Wash thoroughly, boil for six minutes and then fry with bacon - delicious!

Winkles or Periwinkles
(sometimes known as sea-snails)

The removal of the fish from the shell is something of an art in itself! Wash, or soak in water and eat raw. Remember to incarcerate under a lid or they will decamp.

OYSTERS
(FROM THE HELFORD, PERCUIL RIVER AND RIVER FAL)

The harder it is to open the shell, the healthier is the oyster. Do not consume if the shell opens immediately.

Eat raw with a little cayenne pepper and brown bread and butter.

Smoke, for hors d'oeuvres at a cocktail party

Bake in its shell with a little lemon juice and sprinkle with breadcrumbs toasted in butter. Season.

Bake in cream and sherry and grill with breadcrumbs toasted in butter. Do not let the edges of the fish begin to curl. Season.

Oysters are a delicious ingredient for sauce and soup - favourites of the Victorians.

TO ROAST LOBSTERS

Take ye Lobsters alive and as fresh as you can, wash them, clean, lay them fast to ye Spitt and roast them three-quarters of an hour first - basting them with water and white wine vinegar seasoned very well with sweet herbs and onions, whole pepper and a good handful of salt, boil this, then baste ye Lobsters till a little before you draw them, then baste them with butter and salt and shake a little flower over them to make them froth, then draw them, split ye tails and crack ye claws and dish it, having sauce ready, viz., butter, anchovies, a little white wine, nutmeg and small pepper, a blade or two of whole mace, ye juice of a lemon or some vinegar, shake in some flower or crumbs of bread to thicken it, either serve with ye Lobster or in a plate by itself. Garnish with sliced lemon or any green parsley or Horseradish.

Dated 1727
Penzance W.I.

[Taken from 'Cornish Recipes - Ancient and Modern', Edited by Edith Martin and originally published by the Cornwall.Federation of.Womens.Institutes in 1929.]

To Pickle Sprats

Take a Peck of the largest Sprats, without Heads, and Salt them a little over Night; then take a Pot or Barrell, and lay in it a lay of Bay Salt; and then a lay of Sprats, and a few Bay Leaves with a little Lemon Peel, thus do till you have filled the Vessel, then cover and Pitch it that no Air get in set it in a cool Cellar, and once in a week turn it upside down; in three months you may eat them.

Shortlanesend W.I. (This recipe is dated 1698.)

A Trout Pye

Clean, wash and scale them, lard them with Pieces of a Silver Eel rolled up in Spice and sweet Herbs, and Bay Leaves powder'd; lay on and between them the bottoms of slic'd Artichokes, Mushrooms, Oysters, Capers and slis'd Lemon; lay on Butter, and close the Pye.

Truro W.I. (This recipe is dated 1738.)

['To Pickle Sprats' and 'A Trout Pye' are taken from 'Cornish Recipes - Ancient and Modern', edited by Edith Martin and originally published by the C.F.W.I. in 1929.]

Smoked Mackerel Custard

(Serves 3 Persons)

1 Filet of Smoked Mackerel (flaked)	Butter
3 Sticks of Celery (chopped)	Seasoning
3 Eggs	3 teaspoons Cornflour
½ pint Milk	2 tablespoons Double Cream

Place a few knobs of butter in the base of a glass dish and onto this add the flaked mackerel and chopped celery. Mix together. Beat the eggs. Take a small quantity of the beaten egg and mix with 3 teaspoons of cornflour until very smooth. Beat this into the rest of the egg mixture. Season with black pepper and 2 tablespoons of chopped parsley and a pinch of salt. Pour over the fish. Add a little more chopped parsley on top along with the 2 tablespoons of double cream. Bake in a medium-slow oven until just set.

Fish Pie

1½ lbs. fresh filleted Haddock, poached gently in water until it can be flaked. Place a good layer of fish in a casserole and pour over it a little sauce made with a roux to which a little Tomato Sauce or grated Cheese has been added. Continue in layers of fish and sauce, topping with sauce. Cover with grated Cheese and bake in a medium oven until the Cheese has melted on the top and is beginning to brown.

Comford Fish Pie
(from the fox and hounds)

1lb. Coley Fish	14 ozs. tin chopped Tomatoes
½ lb. Cod loin	Pernod to taste
8 ozs. Prawns	Tablespoon of Capers
1 Onion, chopped	4 ozs. fresh Spinach (chopped)
1 Clove Garlic, crushed	1lb. Puff Pastry
2 tablespoons of Olive Oil	Seasoned Flour
Fennel Seeds to season	Teaspoon fresh Dill
Teaspoon fresh Basil	Parsley

Cut fish into chunks and toss in seasoned flour. Heat oil in pan, soften onion and garlic. Do not brown onion because it will become bitter. Stir in dill and basil and cook for a minute. Add the seasoned and floured fish to pan and toss without breaking it up too much. Add the chopped tomatoes and pour the Pernod over, to taste. Adjust taste (for example, the Pernod and fennel seeds). Stir in finely chopped spinach and the capers. Cook for about 5 minutes. Allow to cool and then top with puff pastry (or creamed potatoes) and bake until pastry is golden brown. This may also be eaten cold.

Mrs. Swiss, Fox and Hounds,
Comford,
Near Gwennap.

[Editor: This recipe has been especially constructed by Mrs. Swiss for this book. I have tasted a test sample and it's jolly good and I am told it may appear on the regular menu.]

West Country Folksong:
Child's Verses for Winter

Devon was white,
But Cornwall was green,
Uncommonest sight
That ever was seen.

When Cornwall was copper
Devon was gold:
On moorland and hilltop,
Pasture and fold.

When Devon was purple
Cornwall was brown,
With harvesting bracken
On ledra and down.

When Cornwall was grey
With sea-mist and spume,
Devon was greenest
With apples in bloom.

Devon was shrouded
With snow on each thing,
But Cornwall was verdant
With promise of spring.

A. L. Rowse.

*Messrs. N. Rowe, Fore Street, St. Blazey.
From a New Year's Greeting Card for 1908.*

Lent Assizes
1605

The following is a list of the food purchased for the entertainment of the Judge, Barristers, Grand Jury and Sheriffs Troop for the Lent Assizes in 1605. The Sheriffs Troop included trumpeters and mounted soldiers for the protection of the Judge.

The High Sheriff of Cornwall for 1604-1605 was Francis Godolphin and for 1605-1606 was Nicholas Prideaux. It is most likely that the High Sheriff responsible for the payment of these accounts would have been Nicholas Prideaux and it is probable that he would have taken office on Lady Day, (25th March), 1605 in time for these Lent Assizes.

Imp'imis of wheate 26 bushells	£8 10s.	Rabbetts 50 Cuppell	£3
Beere, 16 hoggsedds	£8	Neates Tonges 40	40s.
Renish wyne & muscadyne 10 gallons a smale Barrell of ech 20 of Renish		Chickens 6 dozen	40s.
		Henns 30	30s.
Clarett wyne 2 hogsetts	£8	Pidgens 40 paier	20s.
Seck a Barrell	£4	Partridges 4 dozen	40s.
One Beefe	£6	Pecocks 4	13s. 4d.
Veles 12	£6	Venyson 6 doe	
Muttons ten	£10	Gammons of Bacon 1	24s.
Lambes 20	£4	Vestfalia Bacon 4 if theye maie bee hadd	
Brawne	30s		
Porks 3	£3	Foule	£5
Rosting Piggs 20	40s.	Pickell Lemmons a barrell	
Turkies 20	40s.	Ollives a Jarr	
Capons 100	£5	Capers 6lb	
		Sampier 3 gallons	

London Linge 6	24s.	Eggs 1000	20s.
Cornish Lying a burthen & half	40s.	Sugar 40lb. waight	£3
		pepper 6lb.	12s.
the lyke quantitie of Mylwyn	40s.	Mace a pownd	20s.
		Cloves 2 pownd	20s.
Buckhorne a hundredd & half	12s.	Nuttmeggs 2 pownd	20s.
Newland fish 100	8s.	Ginger 2 pownd	3s.
Newland Corr fishe	12s.	Synnamon 2 pownd	10s.
Congers 12	43s.	Saffron an ownce	5s. 4d.
A Barrell of herringe	20s.	Reasons half a hundred	20s.
Salt Samons 10	40s.	Prunes a 100 waight	20s.
Fresh Samons 8	40s.	Corrans half a hundred	25s.
Redd hearing	5s.	Sugar for Wyne	30s.
Spratts 400	12s.		
puffyns 24	5s.	howse rent	£10
Anchovyes	5s	wood	£3
Oisters 6000	20s.	Chayrecoale	16s.
Crabbs & Lobsters	20s.	Torches	12s.
fresh fish of all sorts by Sea & Land	£5	Lynkes 2 dozen	8s.
		Candells	40s.
Sturgeon 2 keggs		Trumpetters	40s.
Salt yeeles 40		Cooks 8	£8
Butter 24 gallons	£4	Judges men	
fresh Butter 100 waight	33s.	horsemeate	£8
Creame 20 gallons	50s.	Quinces pears & Apples	£8

[These accounts are taken from the Mount Edgcumbe papers, held at the Cornwall County Record Office. Ref. No.: ME 2846.]

Penponds House Turkey

(Sufficient for 65 people and ideal for Buffet Luncheon Parties, Garden Parties and Wedding Breakfasts.)

Roast 2 or 3 Turkeys (totalling approximately 34 lbs. in weight) and when cold, cut into sizeable chunks.

Place Turkey meat into a large bowl (e.g. bread pancheon) or two smaller bowls. Half fill a large jam kettle or ham kettle with thick white sauce (made with roux using butter and in part Ideal Milk).

Add to this, 1 large can of Peaches and 2 small cans of Apricots - chopping the fruit finely and further adding their juices. Continue by adding: Salt; Ginger; Herbs; Mustard; Soft Brown Sugar; Mayonnaise; a little Vinegar; (Garlic); Basil; Clotted Cream and Wine to taste.

When the sauce is constructed to your liking, allow it to go cold and then pour over the turkey and gently fold in. It is suggested that you might garnish with grapes and almonds.

N.B. These are the main ingredients. It is of great importance to taste at all stages and adjust the flavour to your preference.

Mrs. Fraser Annand,
Treviskey.

Cornish Sausage

½ lb. Minced Beef	1 - 3 teaspoons Tomato Sauce
¼ lb. Minced Bacon	1 Egg
Teacup of Breadcrumbs	Salt
1 or 2 Onions - chopped	Pepper
1 - 3 teaspoons Chutney	Other flavourings to taste.

Mix all these ingredients together. Roll into a sausage shape and wrap closely. Steam for 1½ hours.

Jellied Rabbit

(Wartime Recipe - Second World War)

1 Rabbit	Spice:	4 Cloves
1lb. Steak		1 Stick Cinnamon
2 Eggs		2 Pieces of Mace
Gelatine		All-spice
Salt to taste		(Tie spices in
Pepper		muslin bag)

Cover the rabbit and steak with water and add the spices, salt and pepper. Simmer until tender - this may take about 5 hours. When done, remove all the bones. Soak 2 sheets of gelatine in the gravy and add to the rabbit and steak. Hard boil the eggs and cut into pieces. Place the pieces of egg around the mould and pour in the meat and gravy. Leave to cool and set.

Jugged Hare

1 Hare (joint and retain the blood)	½ bottle Burgundy
8 ozs. fat Bacon	Lemon Peel
1oz. Butter	Black Pepper or Cayenne Pepper
Flour	Salt
6 Cloves	Mixed Herbs
6 ozs. Field Mushrooms	A little Ginger
2 dessertspoons of Tomato purée	Port Wine
3 Onions stuck with Cloves	Little Vinegar

Joint the hare and retain the blood. Cut the bacon into fairly small but thick pieces and chop the onions. Lightly fry in the butter. Seal and brown the meat in the saucepan and sprinkle the flour over the meat and onions. Brown the flour but keep stirring. Place all in a fireproof casserole or heavy lidded pan. Add the wine, tomato purée, mushroom pieces, seasonings and herbs and half to one teaspoon of ginger. Make up liquor with water to cover meat and cook slowly for

3-3½ hours, until the hare is tender. Remove any excess fat. Take the blood and stir in a little vinegar, to prevent it coagulating, and a small quantity of the gravy. Add this to the casserole with a little port. Heat to near boiling but do not let it boil or the blood may curdle.

Serve with Forcemeat balls (see recipe under 'Stuffings').

K. F A.

MARKET DAY SPECIAL

6 Pork Chops	1 small Apple
2 Pig's Kidneys	1 teaspoon dried Sage
2 lbs. Onions	2 tablespoons Tomato Sauce.
1½ lbs. Potatoes	Salt, Pepper.

Peel and slice the potatoes and onions. Put in a casserole dish in layers with the chops and sliced kidneys. Add chopped apple and tomato sauce. Sprinkle with the sage. Cover with a layer of potatoes. Pour over a teacup of water. Season as required. Put well fitting lid on casserole in slow oven and cook 2-3 hours.

CHICKEN AND PORK BRAWN

1 Old Fowl	Pepper and Salt
2 Pig's feet and hocks	Herbs

Skin the fowl, clean it and cut up the joints. Clean the feet and hocks. Put all the meat in a pan of cold water and bring it to the boil. Simmer gently for four hours then strain and remove all bones. Cut up all the meat finely and season highly with pepper and salt. Add some herbs to your taste. Mixed herbs with marjoram is good. Boil all again for 10-15 minutes, then press into a mould and leave to set.

Genuine Cornish Pasty

[The Editor is very grateful to Miss Wendy Eathorne for so kindly granting permission to publish her 'Genuine Cornish Pasty' which first appeared in a Royal Academy of Music Cookery book entitled 'Cooking in Harmony'.]

To make 4 medium-sized pasties, you will need:

1½ lbs. best Steak, or Skirt	1 Kidney
1¼ lbs. Short Crust Pastry	1 beaten Egg
4 smallish Potatoes	Parsley
1 Swede	Salt and Pepper
1 Onion	Knobs of butter

Cut the meat into small pieces. Roll the pastry into 4 circles of about 10" diameter. Cover the top half of the circles with snipped potatoes and add snipped swede and finely chopped onion. Cover with the raw meat and kidney. Add the parsley, salt and pepper and knobs of butter. Fold the bottom half of the pastry circles over the top half, and crimple the edges. Brush with beaten egg. Bake in a hot oven for 5 minutes, and then at moderate heat for 40 minutes.

Miss Wendy Eathorne.

[Editor: Pasties came in many different guises - please see the article entitled 'Fish, Foods, Famines and Fables'.]

Chicken Galantine

1 good sized Fowl	Grated rind of ½ lemon
1lb. Sausage meat	2 ozs. Breadcrumbs
6 ozs. Ham or Tongue	A little Mixed Herbs
2 hard boiled Eggs	1½ pints of Stock
1 raw Egg	Glaze with liquid
Pepper and Salt	Aspic Jelly
Chopped Parsley	Garnish

Clean, draw and bone the fowl. Make a stuffing with sausage meat, breadcrumbs, seasoning and herbs mixed with the beaten egg. Cut the ham into small pieces and quarter the hard boiled eggs. Place all this inside the fowl, sew it up and roll it in a clean muslin or cheesecloth, lightly tied on. Bring the stock to boiling point and put in the stuffed fowl. Simmer for about $2^{1}/_{2}$ hours. When cold, remove the cloth and glaze the whole bird with the liquid aspic jelly. Dish up with a border of lettuce, cress and thinly sliced red pepper. Garnish with aspic jelly, chopped.

Pork Tenderloin Fillet in a Mead and Cider Sauce

1lb. Pork Tenderloin
2 Onions (finely sliced)
4 Carrots (cut into thin strips - Julienne)
$^{1}/_{2}$ lb. Mushrooms (cut into quarters)
$^{1}/_{2}$ pint Cornish Mead
$^{1}/_{2}$ pint Medium Dry Cider
$^{1}/_{2}$ pint Cream (double)
1 Tablespoon Olive Oil
1 Tablespoon Plain Flour

1. Slice the pork into $^{1}/_{2}$" rounds and flatten with the hand.
2. Sauté in half the oil - put to one side when sealed and save juices in the pan.
3. Sauté vegetables in the remaining oil for a few minutes, then remove with a slotted spoon.
4. To this pan, add the meat juices and flour; cook into a roux.
5. Add the mead and cider and bring to the boil.
6. Add the meat and vegetables and bring back to the boil, then simmer. Add cream and continue to simmer until tender.
7. Season to taste. Serve with fresh vegetables or green salad. Enough for 4 persons.

Mrs. Grey,
The Maltsters Arms,
Chapel Amble,
Nr. Wadebridge.

Jugged Steak

A thick piece of Steak
2 Onions
Celery

Cloves
Some Mushroom Ketchup
Pepper and Salt

Cut up the steak into 1 inch squares and put into a stone jar. Add the onions - stuck with cloves, the ketchup, chopped celery, pepper and salt. Cover the jar closely. Place in a pan of boiling water and simmer continuously until the meat is tender. Add no water or fat. Alternatively the ingredients can be put in a lidded casserole and stewed for 2 hours.

Sweet Pickled Pork

1 small leg or hand of Pork
3 ozs. Coarse Salt
3 ozs. Bay Salt

½ pint Ale
½ pint Stout
½ oz. Saltpetre

Put meat in crock and rub well with coarse salt. Then mix well the rest of the salt, the bay salt and the saltpetre. Put the mixture in a saucepan with the ale and stout and bring to the boil, stirring often. Pour the liquid, while boiling hot, over the pork. Turn the pork over, basting well, every day for 14 days. It is then ready to boil or bake as desired. Delicious eaten hot or cold.

Christmas Spiced Beef

About 15 lbs. of beef -
(boneless if possible)
1 oz. Bay salt
8 ozs. Demerara Sugar
1 oz. Saltpetre

2 ozs. Black pepper
¼ oz. Jamaica pepper
½ oz. Cloves
Salt

Well rub the beef all over with salt, bay salt, sugar and saltpetre. Cover with the ground peppers and stick the cloves into the meat.

Leave in a cool place on a large plate or dish and turn and baste with the liquor every day. When ready, in about 3 weeks, remove the cloves and roast in the oven until tender and delicious.

GAMMON AND APRICOT PIE

1 Rasher of Gammon an inch thick	6 Potatoes
½ lb. dried Apricots	Pepper
1oz. Sultanas	A little Gravy

Lightly brown the gammon on both sides in a frying pan, then put in a large pie dish. Put the apricots, previously soaked in water overnight, on the top and sprinkle over some black pepper. Add the sultanas and pour in a little gravy made in the frying pan in which the gammon was browned. Cover with sliced potatoes. Put greaseproof paper over and bake in moderate oven for 1 hour.

ALE HOUSE KIDNEYS
(IN CREAM AND BRANDY SAUCE)

3 ozs. Lamb's Kidneys (quartered)
3 fl.ozs. Whipping Cream
1 Tablespoon Brandy
Knob of Butter

Serves one!

Method:

1. Halve kidneys, remove the core and then quarter them.
2. Heat butter in pan.
3. Sauté kidneys on high heat for 4-5 mins, until cooked.
4. Add cream and bring to simmering point.
5. Add brandy and simmer for 1 minute.
6. Garnish with chopped parsley and serve with Granary Bread and Butter.

[Editor: In the words of the Landlord - "PROPER JOB!" I agree with him; I have eaten this recipe on lots of occasions and thoroughly recommend it. I am grateful to Mr. Keir for allowing me to 'winkle' out the ingredients.]

Mr. and Mrs. Alex. Keir, Old Ale House, Quay Street, Truro.

Mother's Steak and Kidney Pudding

(There is no finer fare for a cold winter meal)

1lb. Shin of Beef	Flour
1/4 lb. Kidney	Dripping
2 Onions	Salt & Pepper to taste

Cut up the beef and kidney into chunks. Toss in the flour and fry in dripping very slowly. Add 2 chopped onions, the seasoning and a little water - nothing else.

To make the suet Crust:
1lb. Plain Flour   1/2 lb. Suet (shredded)
Salt & Seasoning

Mix together with a little water to form a paste. Roll out and line well greased pudding basin, leaving sufficient suet crust to cover the top of the bowl. Three-quarters fill a lined basin with meat and place on top crust. Damp the edges and pinch securely all round.

Cover suet crust with well greased greaseproof paper to fit closely round the inside of the top of the basin. Closely cover pudding with 2 layers of tin-foil, making sure that there is a pleat in the middle. Tie the foil tightly with string against the top ridge of the basin, adding a string handle.

Pressure cook according to size of pudding and instructions of manufacturer.

Serve pudding with a clean napkin around the basin.

Mrs. Fraser Annand,
Treviskey.

Lan'cen (Launceston) Pie

Pieces of meat placed at the bottom of a pie dish, seasoned with pepper and salt then sliced potatoes to nearly fill the dish, more seasoning, and a little water. Add a few small whole potatoes on the top and a roll of pastry as a ring of crust around the edge of this dish. Bake under a kettle in the open chimney.

The round "hearth" was set on a heap of hot ashes, the pie put on it, and a baking "kettle" turned over it; then a ring of ashes where the "hearth" and the "kettle" met, to keep out the smoke. Then furze was piled on and fired until thought to be enough, when a heap of "bruss" (the dust of the furze rick) was heaped on to smoulder and retain the heat.

I have often seen the cook put the fire-hook (for handling the furze) on the edge of the "hearth" and bend to listen if the pie was boiling. This mode of listening for sounds was common.

I have heard an old man telling how, in his boyhood, they listened with the hook on the hearthstone in the days when Napoleon was a terror, and his landing on the coast dreaded at every little cove, fearing to hear the rap of his soldiers and the rolling of their drums.

[Taken from 'Cornish Recipes - Ancient and Modern', edited by Edith Martin and originally published by the C.F.W.I. in 1929.]

GERTY MEAT PUDDINGS

Thoroughly cleanse the inside of a pig with salt and allow it to soak overnight in brine. Take the lights, melt, heart and kidneys, cover with cold water and boil till cooked (¾ hour). Cast down fat and lard, mince scallops and the cooked heart, et cetera. Save the liquid the heart, etc., was boiled in and to every 3 quarts of liquid allow 1 quart groats, and boil till cooked. Add groats to minced ingredients and season with salt and pepper. Fill the skins with this mixture and boil gently ¾ hour.

Pig's blood added to the mixture before putting into the skins makes the above into "Black Pots".

*N.B. "Pots" are the intestines of the pig
St. Mellion W.I.

[Taken from 'Cornish Recipes - Ancient and Modern', edited by Edith Martin and originally published by the C.F.W.I. in 1929.]

Assize Court Menus for Luncheon and Dinner - January 1911

(during the shrievalty of Francis Buller Howell - who was High Sheriff of Cornwall for 1910 - 1911)

Luncheon Menu	Dinner Menu
	(24th. January 1911)
Soup:	
Clear Spring	Soup:
	Clear Oxtail
•	
Lobster in Cases	•
Fillets of Chicken in Aspic	Fish:
Roast Turkey	Filet of Sole, Sauce Tartar
Pressed Beef	
York Ham	•
Ox Tongues	Entrée:
Roast Chicken	Sweet Breads
Game Pie	à la Milanaise
•	•
Trifle	Joint:
Orange Russe	Quarter of Lamb
Velvet Creams	Roast Pheasant
Spring Tarts	Snipe
Wine Jelly	
Fruit Salad	•
	Puddings:
•	Prince of Wales Pudding
Dessert	Italian Cream
•	•
Coffee	Madras Eggs
	•
	Dessert

[Taken from family papers held at the C.R.O.]

Boscawen Street, Truro ~ 1830.

Ruan Lanihorne

Late December, early snow
Round the blunt and sleepy thorn.
Lady, lady will you go
With a twig of mistletoe
To meet your love at Lanihorne?

Every kingfisher you know,
Every quail was bred and born
In the rushes high and low
With minnows in the undertow
In Ruan Ruan Lanihorne.

Lady, lady, when you go
To Lanihorne, to Lanihorne
Thinking yes and thinking no,
Behold emerging from the snow
A little golden Unicorn.

You may see him dance and skip
On the high heraldic foot
While the willows sway and dip
Their swaying, weeping willow-tip
To sounds of the magic flute.

Gently stroke his pointed horn,
Gaze into his jewelled eyes
Ancient, wicked, gay, forlorn.
Give him whiffs of peppercorn
To sniff at till he cries.

And when he's still and out of breath
From dancing, tears and peppercorn
Ask him more and ask him less
Ask about love, life and death
In Ruan Ruan Lanihorne.

And he will answer yes and no
Nodding with his haunted horn.
Lady, lady will you go
With a twig of mistletoe
To meet your love at Lanihorne?

Zofia Ilinska.

The Blunt and Sleepy Thorn at Ruan Lanihorne.

The Story of Saffron

Saffron is as old as the millennium and as new as the age. It is a delicacy of great antiquity which is produced from the red three branched style of the Saffron Crocus (Crocus sativus). The purple flowers are gathered in the early morning as they begin to open and the stigmas and part of the style are hand picked out of the flower head. The wet saffron is then traditionally spread on to sheets of paper to a depth of between two and three inches. These are covered with cloth and a weighted pressing board, sweated by the application of strong heat for a period of two hours followed by gentle heat for a further twenty-four hours. At hourly intervals, the 'cake' is turned to afford even drying.

The Saffron Crocus has long been cultivated in Persia; Kashmir; at the town of Corycus in Cilicia and by the Arabs in Spain since about 961 A.D. It is also grown in France and Sicily and is thought to have been introduced into China at the time of the Mongol invasion. According to the British geographer and sometime Archdeacon of Westminster; Richard Hakluyt, who died in 1616, the Saffron Crocus was brought to England from Tripoli by a pilgrim concealing a stolen corm in the hollow of his staff. Surely a case of corruption in the early Church! It was certainly cultivated at Hinton in Cambridgeshire and at Saffron Walden in Essex; the growers being known as 'Crokers'. It is also mentioned in an English book of leeches in the Tenth Century. The popular belief in Cornwall is that saffron arrived here when the Phoenicians came to trade with the Cornish for tin, but this is probably erroneous as the street vendors' cry of 'Safforn' was a familiar sound to the Fifteenth Century Londoner.

From earliest time, saffron has been variously used. The Greeks had it strewn in their halls, courts, theatres and baths as a perfume and the streets of Rome were sprinkled with saffron for the entry and progress through the city by Nero. In those days it was a Royal colour. The ancient Kings of Ireland had their mantles coloured with saffron dye and we are told that the lein-croich or saffron dyed shirt was worn by the great and the good of the Hebrides as recently as the Seventeenth Century.

As a drug, saffron lent itself to adulteration, for which there existed dire penalties. At Nuremburg, saffron inspections were regularly ordered and in the Fifteenth Century transgressors paid the penalty for their crimes by being burned to death in the market place, along with their bastardised saffron. For a similar crime, following another inspection, three people were buried alive.

The Hindu scholar or Pundit is marked by a sacred spot in part coloured by saffron. It was also used as a glaze upon burnished tinfoil in the production of the gentle art of mediæval illumination, being an inexpensive and successful alternative to gold leaf.

On the subject of etymology, it is thought that the word 'crocodile' derives from the Greek KROCOS = Crocus and DIELOS = timid, feint-hearted or cowardly and hence the old adage 'the crocodile's tears are never true save when he is forced where saffron groweth'. Why is he thus so upset by the innocent crocus? Perhaps a reader may enlighten me.

In the equally gentle art of cookery, it has been used from time immemorial by the Cornish in their saffron cakes and buns. Good saffron should always have a deep orangy-red colour and should it be light yellow or blackish, it is either old or bad. A small quantity goes a long way, which is a good thing as it has always been a very expensive commodity. The old Cornish maxim is well known - 'As dear as saffron'. In 1929 the price was 6/10 (34.16p.)per oz. This was the grocer's price, who sold saffron in Avoirdupois measurements. (Saffron could also be purchased at the chemist in Apothecaries measure). 1oz. Avoirdupois = 28.35 metric grammes. Today (April 1994), Saffron is £1.50 per metric gramme. This means that an ounce of Saffron has increased to £42.52 per oz. over 65 years. - an increase of 12,447%! Saffron is zero rated for Value Added Tax, because it is a foodstuff. Saffron is subject to V.A.T. if it is used for dyeing. The majority now comes from Spain (with a little from Greece and India) and quality is very carefully checked before purchase by the chemist. Adulteration may still occasionally occur by the addition of glycerine and weight may include grasses and stones. The chemist did not know if the modern adulterant still lives in mortal fear of the fire or the sod!

For the growing of saffron, I can do no better than to quote a description taken from an old book dated 1698:

> *"Saffron is a great Improver of Land and will grow in indifferent good Ground, where it is not too Stony or too Wet and in this case having Ploughed your Ground into Ridglands, as for Corn or Pease, take your Roots (a Bushel of which will set an Acre) and having drawn a Drill with a large Hoe, place them therein with the Spurns downwards about three inches asunder; then draw another Drill, so that the Mold of it may cover up the former and in that place others in the same manner and so successively, till you have set your Roots and when they Spring up, draw Earth about them and these you must set in the beginning of July and if the Weather be exceedingly dry you may sometimes water the top ranges and in September the Blew Flower appears and in it upon opening three or four Blades of Saffron which you must observe to gather out Morning and Evening for a Month together, the Flowers continually encreasing.*
>
> *The Saffron being gathered, you must make a Kiln, about half the bigness of a Bee Hive, of Clay and Sticks and so putting a gentle Fire of Charcoal under it, tend it by often turning, till you have reduced three pound of wet Saffron to one of dry; and in this case one Acre of Saffron will amount to between the value of Forty and Fifty pounds in Money, the two Crops,*

for the Roots will yield effectually no more, without being renewed or transplanted and thus much for the improvement of Land, by these profitable means and methods".

Not being a mathematician and not being able to discover how many pounds of English saffron were produced to the acre in 1698, I am unable to deduce the equivalent value of an acre of English saffron at today's prices. The Ministry of Agriculture Fisheries and Food have no information at all with regard to the growing of saffron and tell me that they can find no trace of the crop having been grown commercially in England this century. They have consulted their records back to 1900. It is, however, interesting to note that 1 ounce sold today, equals the whole value of two crops grown on one acre in 1698

Most traditional recipes for Saffron Cake suggest that 1 drachm is required. ($1/16$ th. of an ounce - Avoirdupois). This will cost approximately £2.66 today.

If, having purchased your saffron, you remain strong enough for further activity - seize a pair of scissors and shred the saffron very finely. Pour on half a cup of boiling water and steep over night. The Tincture of Saffron is then added to the flour when making the dough.

One cannot help but wonder how much of this Royal substance is applied to the construction of the shop bought Saffron Cake!

Mrs. Penhaligon's Saffron Cake
(and White Cake)

2½ lbs. Flour
1lb. Butter & Lard mixed
¼ lb. Soft Brown Sugar
1lb. Currants
6 ozs. Lemon Peel

1oz. Yeast
Pinch of Salt
Saffron and Nutmeg to taste
Warm Milk

Mix flour and salt and rub in the butter. Add sugar, currants and peel and mix all together. Put the yeast into a little warm milk and pour into hole in the flour. When it sponges, mix well into the rest of the ingredients, adding more warm milk, with saffron and nutmeg to taste. Beat very well, then put dough into well buttered tin, place in hot oven and bake for about an hour.

"I remember my Grandmother, Mrs. Penhaligon, spreading the saffron on a piece of greaseproof paper and putting it in the oven to dry out. She then soaked it in warm salt water overnight. (Adding only a pinch of salt to the water). She also baked White Cake - which was exactly the same recipe, but without the saffron."

Mrs. Webber, Lanner.

Great Great Aunt Eliza's Christmas Rum Cake

(This is based on an 18th. Century Recipe)

1lb. Butter
1lb. Caster Sugar
1¼ lb. Fine Self Raising Flour
½ lb. Mixed Peel

1lb. Currants
1lb. Sultanas
½ lb. Glacé Cherries
10 Eggs
2 Wine Glasses of Rum

Steep fruit in alcohol over night. Cream butter and sugar - beat eggs and add to mixture. Beat in flour, followed by fruit. Place three layers of greased paper in a baking tin and fill with mixture. Bake for about 5 hours in a slow oven.

N.B. Half quantities can be used for a smaller cake, cooking for about 2 1/2 hours in a slow oven. It is very beneficial to place a bowl of water in the bottom of the oven to assist the retention of moisture in the cake whilst cooking.

[Editor: This is thought to have come from Mary Trezize, who married at Phillock on the 8th. October 1792. Her daughter married John Tredinnick and he was Great Great Aunt Eliza's Grandfather.]

TREDINNICK BLACK CAKE

[This is an 18th. Century recipe which has been used in our family for at least the last five generations. Editor]

2 lb. Currants	6 ozs. Cherries (halved)
1/2 lb. Plain Flour	1/2 lb. Ground Almonds
3/4 lb. Butter	2 teaspoons Carbonate of Soda
4 Eggs	1/2 teaspoon Almond Essence
1/2 lb. Dark Brown Sugar	1/4 teaspoon Mixed Spice
(or Caster Sugar)	1 tablespoon Molasses
1/2 lb. Candied Peel	Brandy

Put all fruit in bowl and soak in good quantity of brandy. Stir well. Place a plate over the fruit to press gently and cover the bowl closely with a cloth. Leave to steep overnight. Mix well together, the butter; sugar and ground almonds. Add beaten eggs - one at a time with a tablespoon of flour to prevent curdling. Add molasses to mixture and beat in. Add spice and carbonate of soda to the remainder of the flour and gradually add to mixture, beating all the time. Then add 1/2 teaspoon of almond essence and mix again. Now add all steeped fruit and mix with wooden spoon until all is combined.

Line large cake tin with two sheets of newspaper followed by two sheets of greaseproof paper. Grease well and place mixture in tin. Cook in slow oven for 3 1/2 - 4 hours.

N.B. Place a dish of water on the floor of the oven to keep cake moist. Do not open range door for at least 3 hours and then only very gently.

Mock Almond Tartlets

(Wartime recipe - Second World War)

Shortcrust Pastry
3 ozs. Butter (or any available fat)
3 ozs. Sugar
1 Egg
2 tablespoon Soya Flour
Almond Essence
Raspberry Jam

Line tartlet tins with pastry and add a little raspberry jam. Slightly warm the butter and sugar and mix well. Add the beaten egg and almond essence followed by the soya flour. Beat thoroughly. Place a little mixture in each pastry case and bake in a moderate oven for 15 - 20 minutes.

[Editor: On the subject of wartime egg rationing, the following is an amusing tale told me by an old woman, of life up country:

"I was going up Coventry during the war and stayed visitin'. There was some awful rationin' and 'ow they poor dears did live, I dunno. One day I saw a maid drop 'er one egg for the week - that's all they was allowed - outside the butcher's shop and oh! my dear life, there were such a confloption. She d'give a great shout and runned in to get a saucer to save the yolk. But she was clever see and shovelled the yolk onto the saucer and gived it to the butcher - 'andsome fella. He was some pleased and did give 'er 'arf a sausage extra with 'er four ounces o' meat".]

Violet Cake

4 ozs. Butter
4 Eggs
2 ozs. Ground Rice
1 teaspoon Baking Powder
Crystallized Violets

4 ozs. Caster Sugar
¼ lb. Flour
Vanilla Essence
A little Milk

Cream the butter and sugar. Add the eggs, well beaten, and mix. Stir in the flour, ground rice, a few drops of vanilla and baking powder, with milk to moisten.

Pour half the mixture into a well greased tin. Add a layer of chopped peel and glacé cherries. Pour in the rest of the mixture.

Bake in a moderate oven. When cold, marzipan, ice and decorate with crystallized violets.

Mrs. Wallen, Hayle.

Pat's Cider Cake

8 ozs. Self-Raising Flour	2 Eggs
5 ozs. Margarine	7½ tablespoons Cider
5 ozs. Sugar	Salt

Cream the margarine and the sugar together. Add the beaten eggs, salt, flour and cider.

Cook for 2 hours in a slow oven.

Auntie Ethel's Hot Apple Cake

6 ozs. Self Raising Flour	4 ozs. Currants
3 ozs. Butter	2 Eggs
1 cup of Chopped Apple	4 ozs. Caster Sugar
1oz. Brown Sugar	A little Icing Sugar
1oz. Butter	

Rub the butter into the flour. Stir in the currants, caster sugar and apple. Mix to a soft dough with the egg. Put in a greased shallow tin and cook in a medium oven until golden brown. Place on a hot dish.

Split and spread with 1oz. butter and the brown sugar. Dust with icing sugar.

(Miss Ethel Tredinnick's recipe.)

Mother's Hazelnut Gateau

This makes a wonderful and exotic cake for a special tea or as pudding for a dinner party and is highly recommended.

For Meringue:
> 6 White of Eggs
> 12 ozs. Caster Sugar
> 3 ozs. Ground Almonds
> 3 ozs. Hazelnuts - chop finely but leave a few larger pieces
> Rice Paper

Other Ingredients:
> 8 ozs. Plain Chocolate
> Knob of Butter
> About 1 tablespoon Water
> 1 pint Whipped Double Cream
> Small tin of Pineapple Rings or Chunks

Whisk the 6 whites to a stiff consistency. Add half the sugar and whisk again - the mixture should form peaks. Fold in the rest of the sugar gently, followed by the mixed nuts. Line four Swiss-roll tins with non stick baking paper (if not available, lightly buttered greaseproof paper). Next, place a piece of rice paper in each tin to fit and coat each piece with a quarter of the mixture. Cook very slowly until crisp. When the meringues are cool, but not cold, gently turn each tin upside down on a baking board and peel off the baking paper or greaseproof. The rice paper should adhere to the meringues. Allow to get cold, then carefully turn one meringue the right way up on to an oblong dish. Melt the chocolate very gently with about a tablespoon of water and a knob of butter, stirring all the time and spread a layer over each meringue, followed by a layer of whipped cream, to all except the fourth meringue. Sandwich the layers together, the top layer being covered with chocolate only. Chop up the drained pineapple and mix with the remaining cream. Cover the top of the cake thickly.

This recipe is also delicious made with raspberries instead of pineapple.

Mrs. Fraser Annand,
Treviskey.

Womens' Institute, Truro – Two Day Bazaar, 1919.

Bread & Bread Rolls

3 lbs. strong white Flour
$3/4$-1oz. Lard
8 fluid ozs. milk
Water

2-3 teaspoons Salt
$1^{1}/_{2}$ ozs. fresh Yeast
[or $^{1}/_{2}$-$^{3}/_{4}$ oz. dried yeast]
1 teaspoon sugar

Place flour and salt in Bread Pancheon and rub in the lard. Place to warm.

In two jugs, place in each 4 fluid ozs. of milk made up to 12 fluid ozs. with luke warm water. Crumble half the yeast into each jug, add $^{1}/_{2}$ a teaspoon of sugar to each and stir up. Stand in a warm place until the yeast froths. [For dried yeast add 3-4 teaspoonfuls into each jug].

When the flour is warm, make a hollow in the centre and add the yeast in milk and water. Add further warm water as required to make a creamy dough.

Knead with the base of the hands, pulling and stretching the dough out sideways and then folding in each end and repeating for between 5-10 minutes.

Cover the pancheon with a cloth and place in a warm and draught free place near the range to rise until the dough has doubled in size (between 1-$1^{1}/_{2}$ hours depending upon the temperature of the room - which should always be warm).

Knock the dough back and knead again for a further 3-5 minutes. Form into shapes and place in warmed and greased (with lard) bread tins or on warmed and greased baking tins if you are making rolls. Wait for dough to rise, until it has doubled in size again. Sprinkle tops lightly with flour.

Cook in a moderately hot range [if cooking with electricity 450°-475°F, 200°-250°C for first 10 minutes then reduce temperature]. Bread will take up to $^{3}/_{4}$ of an hour and rolls about 20-25 minutes. Do not open the oven door to check progress until half the cooking time has elapsed.

Grandma Hutchen's Raspberry Puffs

2 ozs. each of Caster Sugar and Butter
1 Egg
$1/2$ teaspoonful of Baking Powder
1 tablespoonful of Flour
1 packet of Birds Blancmange powder (Raspberry Flavour)

Stir the butter and sugar together for a few minutes, add the egg and by degrees the flour; baking powder and blancmange powder. Put into well-greased puff pans or tartlet tins and bake for 7 to 10 minutes. If preferred when nearly baked, put in the centre of each a teaspoonful of raspberry jam and then return to the oven to finish baking.

Spiced Buns

1lb. Flour	6 ozs. Fat
6 ozs. Sugar	8 ozs. Currants
$1/4$ teaspoon Mixed Spice	$1/2$ teaspoon Baking Powder
1 Egg	A little Milk

Amalgamate ingredients. Form into bun-like balls and place on a greased baking tin, allowing room to spread. Bake in a moderate oven.

Cornish Lemon Drizzle Cake

4 ozs. soft Butter or Margarine	4 tablespoons milk
6 ozs. Caster Sugar	Grated rind of 1 Lemon
6 ozs. Self-Raising Flour	Syrup:
Pinch Salt	3 tablespoons Icing Sugar
2 Eggs (size 3)	Juice of 1 Lemon (warmed)

Method:

1 Grease and line a suitable cake tin. (7")

2 Mix all the cake ingredients together to form a soft dropping consistency.

3   Place into a 2lb. loaf tin and bake for 45-55 minutes in a moderate oven.

4   Remove from the oven. Cool slightly and prick with a fork.

5   Mix the icing sugar and lemon juice together and drizzle over the cake.

6   Leave until cold then turn out and serve.

N.B. cooking times will vary if alternative tins are used.

Mrs. Lester Bolitho, Penzance.

CORNISH HEAVY CAKE

1lb. Self Raising Flour
½ lb. Butter
2 ozs Caster Sugar
¾ lb. Currants

Grated Rind of 1 Lemon
Pinch of Salt
Milk to mix

Mix flour, salt and sugar and add the butter, cut into small pieces. Stir this around so that the butter is well distributed, then add the fruit and lemon peel and mix to stiff dough with milk. Roll out to an oblong. Then roll up the dough and place in refrigerator for about ½ hour. Next, take out and roll to an oblong about 1-1½ inches thick. Place on a baking tray and criss-cross the cake with a knife (diamond shapes). Sprinkle liberally with granulated sugar and bake in a good oven for about ¾ hour. When baked, a little caster sugar sprinkled all round the edges adds to the appearance.

CORNISH BOILED CAKE

4 ozs. Margarine
6 ozs. Dark Brown Sugar
12 ozs. Any Dried Fruit
2 ozs. Good Mixed Peel
2 Fl.ozs. Water*
1 level teaspoon Bicarbonate of Soda

1 heaped teaspoon Mixed Spice
2 Beaten Eggs
4 ozs. Plain Wholemeal Flour
4 ozs. Self Raising Wholemeal Flour
Pinch of Salt

*May be substituted in part with Whisky, Rum or Stout.

Place margarine, sugar, fruit, peel, water (or water and alcohol), bicarbonate of soda and spice in a pan and bring to the boil. Simmer for one minute and allow to cool.

Add the beaten eggs, flours and salt. Pour into an 8" round tin and cook in a moderate oven for 1¼ hours.

Mrs. Nicholas St.Aubyn,
Trenowth.

[Editor: Mrs. St.Aubyn adds: "Even I can make it and it tastes excellent and lasts for days! I have used it for Christmas, but also for every day".]

INGREDIENTS FOR A GREAT CAKE

5 lb. Butter brought to a cream	Peel of 2 Oranges
5 lb. Flour	Pint of Canary
3 lb. White Sugar	½ pint Rosewater
7 lb. Currants	43 Eggs (half ye whites)
2/6 worth Perfume (1929?)	1 lb. Citron

St. Mawgan W.I.

Sent by a St. Mawgan member, culled from an old Cookery Book date 1763.

A PENZANCE CAKE

Ingredients:

1 lb. Flour	½ oz. Ground Cinnamon
1 lb. Currants	2 Eggs
½ lb. Ginger	A teaspoonful Baking Soda
¼ lb. Peel	(dissolved in a cup of warm Milk)
¼ lb. Butter	

Cream the butter in the flour and mix in the dry ingredients. Beat the eggs well and stir in with wooden spoon, then the milk. Bake 2½ to 3 hours a slow oven

Polkerris W.I.

['Ingredients for a Great Cake' and 'A Penzance Cake' are taken from 'Cornish Recipes - Ancient and Modern', edited by Edith Martin and originally published by the C.F.W.I in 1929.]

Rationing - Second World War

As the housewives of war-torn England became further ground down by the rigours of rationing, various firms in Southern Ireland (which was a neutral Country) offered with entrepreneurial spirit, various commodities unseen upon the shelves of the English larder. Viz:

Bacon Shops Ltd.,
Provision Merchants,
54, Upper Dorset Street, Dublin.

Apple Jam   1½ lb. tin ....1s. 7½ d.
Plum Jam   1½ lb. tin ....1s. 10½ d.
Red Grape Jam 2lb. tin ....2s. 6½ d.
Seville Orange Marmalade: ½ lb. tin .....2/=
                          2 lb. tin 2/9

All these items could be sent upon receipt of a postal order to include the appropriate postage charges.

Chocolate Grenades

(Wartime recipe - Second World War)

¼ lb. Butter (In the wartime we used a mixture of any fats available)
6 ozs. Self-Raising Flour   3 ozs. Caster Sugar
A little strong Coffee for flavouring*   Cocoa Powder
Plain Chocolate - Two Tuppeny bars

(*During the war we used Camp Coffee - the only coffee available.)

Mix flour and sugar together, rub in the butter and mix to a stiff consistency with a little coffee. Mould the mixture into small half almond shapes with a teaspoon. Place on floured baking sheet. Bake in a moderate oven for about 10 - 15 minutes. When cold, spread each shape on flat side with melted chocolate to which a little coffee has been added. Press the shapes in pairs - flat side together and roll in cocoa powder.

"A friend of mine called Jim Buckman named these cakes Chocolate Grenades, because they reminded him of hand grenades and the name stuck from that day forward".

The War Effort ~ 1914.
11, Boscawen Street, Truro.

An eleven year old boy appeals for help to run the shop.

Puddings, Cakes and Biscuits

Of puddings and cakes there are many delicious recipes within these pages, from the rich and sumptuous Black Cake and other festive fare to the well known figgie hobbin, sometimes figgy duff ('figs is Cornish for ra'sins'). A notice was observed in a shop window earlier this century advertising 'figgie duff 4d. per lb. - more figgier - 5d.!' And then there is Pie Cake which sounds like a colloquialism with a slightly irreligious twist poking fun at what must surely be more properly called Lenten Fast Cake constructed no doubt with a mixture of olives and unleavened bread coloured by Tincture of Permanganate and cooked in sack cloth over a hot ash fire; all ingredients to be purchased, of course, only with Maundy money. What we actually find is that it is another ingenious method of using the age old ingredients in a time honoured way: pastry made with suet (sometimes dripping) and lard cut into two rounds, one at the bottom and one on the top sandwiched together with new potatoes; turnip; onions; seasoning and a little meat, crimped together. Well surely that should be within the fish and meat chapter, you say, and I have to agree. I have nothing in defence save that it was in the 'cake section' of an old Cornish recipe book in my ownership and here the 'fish and meat' was full whereas 'puddings and cakes' is somewhat lacking zest! Now there's a thought for a new ingredient in the Pie Cake.

But what is the traditional Cornish cake? I suppose if one had to be chosen by means of a straw pole by the visitor, it would have to be the Saffron Cake, of which I have at least ten recipes. I have covered, in depth, the subject of saffron within this anthology and recommend strongly that you bake one and try the real thing. Another traditional Cornish cake is the Heavy Cake. There were also cakes and puddings for special feast days and those specific to locations such as the Penzance Cake and the Helston Pudding. Biscuit recipes included Gingerbreads and Fairings (originally made for the celebration of a specific fair) and we must not forget to mention the Great Cake. This is a recipe included in an ancient cookery book of 1763 and includes: 5 lbs. flour; 7 lbs. currants; 5 lbs. butter; 3 lbs. sugar; 2/6 worth of perfume (in 1929) and other ingredients culminating in 43 eggs, but as a great and helpful saving - only 'half ye whites!' Why not try it and then you could also start a meringue stall at no extra cost, or indulge in the delicious recipe for Hazelnut Meringue Gateau within this volume which can certainly grace the best dinner party table for pud.

It has been said that Cornwall at war was a slight misnomer, save that it sent its fair share of young men to the front and much important work was conducted on the River Fal in and around Tolverne, with regard to the preparations for the D-Day landing. The unusual sight of concrete boats can be seen to this day moored on the river and dating from those times - times that saw many Cornish fishing vessels joining the Armada to France to rescue the soldiers from the beaches.

Rationing, of course, was strictly applied and agriculture was geared to send large quantities of produce which had been grown by armies of land girls, out of the County. Being remote, many evacuees were sent to the Duchy from the industrial towns of Britain and in particular the Capital - even the choir of Truro Cathedral was augmented with that of St. Paul's! This no doubt placed added strains upon the housewife even with the extra ration book supplied by the evacuee in question. Always resourceful, the Cornish cook turned her thoughts to ways of producing something out of nothing. We include a taste of various war time recipes, (some of which are jolly good), as an interesting reminder of that period in the county's history - along with a few amusing anecdotes.

CLOTTED CREAM

Use new milk and strain at once, as soon as milked, into shallow pans. Let it stand for 24 hours in winter and 12 hours in summer. Then put the pan on the stove, or, better still into a steamer containing water, and let it slowly heat until the cream begins to show a raised ring around the edge. When sufficiently cooked place in a cool dairy and leave for 12 or 24 hours. Great care must be taken in moving the pans, so that the ream is not broken, both in putting on the fire and taking off. When required skim off the cream in layers into a glass dish for the table, taking care to have a good "crust" on the top. Clotted cream is best done over a stick fire.

[Taken from 'Cornish Recipes - Ancient and Modern', edited by Edith Martin and originally published by the C.F.W.I. in 1929.]

ST. BREOCK PLUM PUDDING

(An 18th. Century Cornish Recipe)

1 lb. Suet
¾ lb. Raisins
1 lb. Currants
½ lb. Sultanas
¾ lb. Mixed Peel
½ lb. Glacé Cherries
      (halved)
¾ lb. Demerara Sugar
2 ozs. Chopped Almonds
(The Glacé Cherries are a later addition)

¾ lb. Breadcrumbs
½ lb. Self Raising Flour
4 teaspoons Mixed Spice
3 Eggs
2-3 tablespoons Syrup
      (or Treacle)
3 tablespoons Rum or
      Brandy
½ pint Porter or Ale

Steep fruit overnight in the spirit. Combine all other ingredients and stir in fruit. Have a wish! Boil each pudding for 8 hours, followed by a further 2 hours on day of eating. (The time is greatly reduced by using a pressure cooker).

[This recipe makes about eight puddings and is a reduction from the original recipe, the quantities of which made about thirty puddings!].

This is a very ancient Tredinnick recipe which has always been known as St. Breock Plum Pudding in our family. Whether it really came from St. Breock we shall never know. The Tredinnicks, (Tredennick, or more anciently Tredeneck), supported the Royalist cause. When Charles II was beheaded in 1679 and Oliver Cromwell became Lord Protector, the Tredeneck family was outlawed and the estates were sold.

The ancient mansion of Tredeneck was spoken of as having been a 'a stately pile of buildings with the hall windows as the largest of the kind in the kingdom'. It was sold to Lord Robartes. His descendant, the Earl of Radnor, owned it in 1736 and it was subsequently purchased by Sir William Molesworth. The house was destroyed many years ago. In St. Breock Parish Church are various monuments to the Tredenecks, the earliest of which is dated 1578 and is a slate stone with a shield of arms of many quarterings. Under this monument are brasses to Charles Tredeneck, a wife and his twelve children. It is believed he may have had two wives, producing seven children by the first and five by the second. In 1531, Christopher Tredeneck of Tredeneck was High Sheriff of Cornwall during the reign of Henry VIII.

Dunveth was also a seat of the family and was sold by Lewis Tredeneck to Robert Wilton, whose grandson conveyed it in 1702 to Sir John Molesworth - in whose family it remained for many years. Dunveth is said to be haunted by a phantom coach and horses.

As the guttering candlelight and the ghostly glow of the dying embers played their nightly tune on the oak panelled bed chambers of Dunveth, the seventeenth century Tredenecks, sequestered in their four poster beds, would have drawn the hangings close to banish the howl of the winter's storm and the unearthly noises of the night. They would have longed for the first watery shafts of morning light to break through the leaded panes in the mullion and banish the powers of darkness. They would also have prayed to the Lord for safe deliverance in the ancient words of the Cornish Litany:

> *From ghosties and goulies*
> *And long leggety beasties*
> *And things that go bump in the night,*
> *Good Lord, deliver us!'*

Victorian Imperial Pudding

2 ozs. Butter
1 oz. Sugar
4 ozs. Breadcrumbs
1 oz. Peel
3 ozs. Raisins

1 Egg
2 tablespoons Syrup
2 tablespoons Milk
Rind of Lemon

Beat the butter and sugar to cream. Add the dry ingredients. Continue by adding the beaten eggs, milk and lemon rind. Place mixture in a suitable pudding basin and steam it for 1½ hours.

N.B. Remember to keep topping up the level of the water.

Muriel's Lemon Curd Sponge Pudding

3 ozs. Breadcrumbs
   (2½ large slices)
½ pint Milk
2 Egg Yolks
2 ozs. Sugar
2 ozs. Butter

Meringue made with:
2 Egg Whites
1oz. Sugar
Lemon Curd

To the breadcrumbs and milk, blend in the egg yolks, sugar and butter. Place in fireproof dish. Cover with lemon curd and meringue. Cook and serve with clotted cream.

Mrs. (Binkie) Wallen, Hayle.

Figgie Hobbin*

Take a little suet, a little lard, teaspoonful baking powder, rub this into ½ lb. flour, add figs[+] to taste. Mix with cold milk or water to a stiff paste. Roll into 4" squares about ½ inch thick. Cut across the top and bake ½ hour.

Perranporth W.I.

*Sometimes called figgy duff. A notice was seen in a shop window not long since, [prior to 1929] - "Figgy Duff   4d. lb., More Figgier,   5d."

[+] *NB "Figs is just Cornish for raisins".*

[Taken from 'Cornish Recipes - Ancient and Modern', edited by Edith Martin and originally published by the C.F.W.I. in 1929.]

Floury Milk

Bring some scald milk to the boil and stir in thickening made of white flour and a good pinch of salt, just as for white sauce. When boiling, sprinkle in some currants and rolled spice, and lightly sweeten with sugar. Pour into basins over small squares of bread.

This was always the correct breakfast on the day when the Great Wheat Stack was carried.

Mullion W.I.

[Taken from 'Cornish Recipes - Ancient and Modern', edited by Edith Martin and originally published by the C.F.W.I. in 1929.]

Gerty Grey

Flour and water boiled together but kept quite thin, season with salt and pepper. Eaten hot.

Tregothnan W.I.

[Taken from 'Cornish Recipes - Ancient and Modern', edited by Edith Martin and originally published by the C.F.W.I. in 1929.]

Gerty Milk*

Flour and water boiled together but kept "runny", season with salt and pepper and eaten hot.

Tregothnan W.I.
> [Taken from 'Cornish Recipes - Ancient and Modern', Edited by Edith Martin and originally published by the C.F.W.I. in 1929.]

> *This is a breakfast dish and used in place of porridge or bread and milk by many people at the present time. [1929.]
> Arising from these there are two old Cornish sayings:
> 'If a man was hacking old stumps he would say: "Gerty grey, if you won't come up, there you may stay"; or "Gerty milk, if you won't come up, I'll break the hilt".'

Chocolate Marquaise

5 ozs. Plain Bourneville Chocolate
10 ½ ozs. softened unsalted Butter
7 egg yolks
8 ¾ ozs. Caster Sugar
5 ¾ ozs. unsweetened Cocoa
18 ozs. Whipping Cream ⎫
1 ¾ ozs. Icing Sugar   ⎬ Chantilly Cream
3 packets of Sponge fingers (about 70 in number)
1 small cup of strong black Coffee (or Camp Coffee) - quantity as desired

1. Melt chocolate.
2. Beat egg yolks and sugar until light and pale.
3. Add melted chocolate and blend.
4. Add together butter and cocoa powder until well blended.
5. Incorporate all together.
6. Make Chantilly Cream by mixing cream and icing sugar together. Fold into mixture.
7. Line oblong foil container with the sponge fingers which have been dipped in the coffee.
8. Carefully add chocolate mixture and when half full add a layer of the sponge fingers. Fill to the top of the tin and cool well before turning out and serving.

Bread and Butter Pudding

Buttered Bread　　　　　Granulated Sugar
Brown Sugar　　　　　　Currants

Sprinkle brown sugar in the bottom of a fireproof dish and cover with a layer of thick strips of buttered bread (butter side up). Cover thickly with currants. Place another layer of buttered bread crossways, leaving space and on this more currants. Continue until dish is full but do not add currants to the top layer of buttered bread.

> Make Custard by taking:
> 4 large eggs - switched up to which add:
> 1 pint warm milk and mix. Then add:
> 2 tablespoons Caster Sugar and
> $1/2$ teaspoon Ground Nutmeg.

Pour the custard through the holes in the top layer of bread but do not fully immerse the top layer. Cover this last layer of bread fairly thickly with granulated sugar. Place in the top oven of range at a moderate heat until just set. Serve with plenty of Clotted Cream - delicious!

This recipe becomes particularly Cornish when made with yesterday's saffron buns or slices of saffron cake instead of bread.

Grandma Hutchens's Christmas Pudding

1lb. Suet　　　　　　　1lb. Sugar
1lb. Breadcrumbs　　　　$1/2$ lb. Peel
1lb. Flour　　　　　　　$1/4$ lb. Almonds
1lb. Currants　　　　　　3 Eggs
1lb. Raisins　　　　　　　Small Tin Spice
Cinnamon　　　　　　　Nutmeg
　　　　　　　　　　　　Baking Powder

Combine ingredients. Place in a lined tin and bake slowly in a moderate oven.

Mr. Lester Bolitho said his Grandmother would not have soaked the fruit in any alcohol because she was a strict Methodist.
[Suggested optional alcohol for steeping: Brandy, Rum or Porter.]

Pancakes Supreme

(Sufficient for 4 pancakes of about 8" diameter each.)

4 ozs Self Raising Flour Milk to mix
1 egg

Sift the flour into a basin, add the eggs and break it up a little. Mix and stir the milk in, a little at a time, breaking up the flour with the back of a spoon against the basin. When sufficient milk has been added to make a very smooth batter of pouring consistency beat very well, raising spoonfuls fairly high and dropping into the basin. This causes bubbles and aerates the mixture. Leave for about 5 minutes, then beat well again. Have ready a pan with a little hot melted lard and pour in enough batter to just cover the pan. Cook fairly quickly, turing the pancake as soon as it is browned and crisp, to cook on the other side.

Fillings:

1 Plain
Dredge with caster sugar, squeeze lemon juice over and roll up. Repeat sugar and lemon juice on top.

2 Sweet fillings
Dredge with caster sugar. Cover the middle with fruit - e.g. sliced peaches, blackcurrants or any fruit you fancy. And turn each side over. Dredge the top with sugar and cover with blobs of clotted cream or thick whipped cream. It is also very good with pineapple jam inside, or a little stem ginger in syrup - cream on top of course!

3 Savoury Fillings - no sugar
  1 Flaked fish in a little sauce - cheese, mayonnaise etc.
  2 Minced meats with a little chutney.
  3 Chopped mixed vegetables lightly cooked first, with a little cheese sauce, celery, et cetera.

Pancake Day

Have you ever tossed a pancake?
Well, it's worth it if you dare
You could make one something special,
Something shatteringly rare.

Now I thought it would be easy
Just a gentle shake - and toss,
And then track it as it travels,
Quickly flip the pan across.

If you're lucky you will catch it
With a whoop of high delight.
But I didn't and it shattered,
Left me pondering my plight.

Undeterred I tried another,
But that ended up in strife,
For it soared right up to heaven
To surrender its young life.

By now I'd got the giggles -
This was foolish fiendish fun!
So I'd make a few more pancakes,
Hit a winner - and then run.

But I sloshed one on the ceiling
And I sloshed one on the walls
And I sloshed the flack descending -
Felt like battering tennis balls.

So my pancake day was over -
One absurd heuristic mess:
I just slumped, convulsed in laughter
I'd enjoyed that game, oh yes!

Marjorie Fraser Annand.

Celtic Delight

This recipe was discovered quite by chance and makes simple and delicious pudding for a dinner party or cakes for afternoon tea.

Firstly: make a rich shortbread to the following recipe:
8 ozs. Plain flour
4 ozs. Rice Flour
8 ozs. Butter
4 ozs. Caster Sugar

Beat well together the sugar and butter; work in gradually, the flour and rice flour, previously combined, until the mixture is completely integrated. Slightly grease a Swiss roll tin and dredge it with rice flour and a little flour - shaking off the surplus. Place the mixture in the tin and knead it down gently with your knuckles until level. With a skewer, punch holes in it. Cook it in a medium oven, lowering the temperature after about 10 minutes. Continue to cook, lowering the temperature again if necessary, until the shortbread is pale, but crisp all through. Dredge lightly with caster sugar and then cut into squares or oblongs whilst still warm. Leave in the tin until cold. Just prior to serving add thickly, one of the following toppings:

1. Gently combine roughly equal quantities of Philadelphia Soft Cheese and Cornish Clotted Cream.
2. To the above ingredients add homemade Kea Plum Jam. (Kea plums, which are very well known in Cornwall, come from Kea, near Truro).
3. To the ingredients of suggestion 1, add homemade Blackcurrant Jam. This is a sharper flavour than the above and particularly good.

In all the above recipes, stir the clotted cream gently to liquefy and break up the crust. Combine cheese and jam (if required) first and then fold in the cream. Do not overwork to prevent the mixture becoming too thick.

M. F A. & K. F A.

Bunching Daffodils on the Isles of Scilly.

An old Scillonian flower farmer with his wife, sons and daughters bunching flowers at Lower Rocky Farm, St. Mary's, in the early days of the industry ~ about 1875.

Helston Flora

On the 15th April 1201, King John granted the first of that which became over the centuries, a total of twenty-four Royal Charters to the Borough of Helston. It is the most shameful disgrace that after nearly 800 years of Chartered Rights and Privileges, the local government re-organisation of 1974 deprived Helston of its Borough status. Helstonians remember the solemn declaration made by Queen Elizabeth I in 1585,

"WE, therefore, considering and of our knowledge holding as certain, that the Borough of Helston is an ancient Borough and one of the most ancient Boroughs in our Duchy of Cornwall.... have willed, ordained and appointed and granted and by these presents for us and our heirs and successors do will, ordain and appoint, grant and declare that the Borough of Helston shall be and remain hereafter a free Borough of itself and that the Burgesses of the Borough hereafter and for ever may and shall be one Body Corporate and Politic in itself, in deed, fact and name, by the name of the Mayor and Commonalty of the Borough of Helston."

E.R.

By what possible trumped-up rights can these grey little men of government overturn 773 years of Royal history, granted in perpetuity by Kings and Queens? It is not surprising that Helstonians deplore their actions - and quite rightly. However, history is not forgotten in that ancient town.

On May 8th each year, (unless that falls on a Sunday or Monday), is Helston Flora Day - an invocation to Spring, the triumph of Life over Death and the passing from Darkness into Light. It is one of the oldest customs of pagan origin still preserved in this Country. The perfect day is a day of warm sunshine and gentle zephyrs. Upon such a day, Flora becomes an harbinger of early summer. It is probable that the oldest part of the days proceedings is the Hal-An-Tow. At first light, the youths gather branches of sycamore. Later, they perambulate through the town waving the branches over their heads and stopping at certain points to sing the Hal-An-Tow song. The early dance of the day precedes this and occurs at 7.00 a.m. The Childrens' Dance is at 10.00 a.m. and the Principal Dance of the day is 12 noon, which is repeated at 5.00 p.m. - the Evening and Last Dance of the Day. The Dance is known as the Furry Dance.

The dances are processional; with order and graceful dignity. The gentlemen wear morning dress and top hats, with buttonholes of lily of the valley; the ladies are in delightful flowing dresses. They dance through the streets and in and out of the houses all bedecked with greenery and spring flowers including bluebells and wild garlic (called 'Scifers') to the time honoured tune played by the Helston Band. A truly magical experience is to hear those distant thumps of the big bass drum and then the gathering strains of the band as the sounds are borne on the breeze to the listening ear. The Victorian setting of 'The Floral Dance' by Katie Moss was made famous by Peter Dawson's rendering on 78 gramophone record. It is this setting which is also responsible for the slightly hackneyed phrase 'a quaint old Cornish town'! As a singer, I have rendered this song on many occasions in recital throughout this Country and abroad. I now realize that the tune played by the band is far less frenetic than the vocal arrangement and holds within its simple harmonies, an old fashioned courtly grace.

Traditional fare on Flora Day is Russian Creams, which would also have been eaten on Christmas Day along with Helston Pudding. I am grateful to Mr. Martin Matthews, of the Helston Folk Museum for supplying, most kindly, these ancient recipes.

To accompany this time honoured fare, why not drop in to the Blue Anchor Inn for a pint of Spingo 'Flora Day Special Brew'? (and I can <u>thoroughly</u> recommend it!) It is brewed on the premises and made from their own well water. I am told by the barman, Tony, that brewing has taken place in the same building since the days when the Blue Anchor was a monks' rest home - and I wonder from what they were resting? In the days when the population of Helston was about five hundred (but when the miners used to get paid in the pubs), there were some thirty brewing houses in the Town.

Should you require something more substantial with your Spingo's than Russian Cream, then the Landlady, Miss Kim Corbett, makes homemade pasties on the premises. A perfect end to a perfect day.

[Information on Flora Day gained from 'The Helston Furry Dance', the official publication of The Flora Day Association.]

HELSTON PUDDING

2 ozs. ($^1/_2$ cup) each of Raisins and Currants
2 ozs. ($^1/_4$ cup) Sugar
2 ozs. (1$^1/_4$ cups) fresh Breadcrumbs
2 ozs. ($^1/_2$ cup) Flour
A pinch of Salt
2 tablespoons ground Rice
2 tablespoons grated Suet
$^1/_2$ teaspoon each of Mixed Spice and Bicarbonate of Soda
6 tablespoons Milk
1 tablespoon finely chopped Peel

Dissolve the soda in the milk, mix all the dry ingredients together and then add the soda and milk. Pour into a well-greased basin, cover with greased paper and either boil (with hot water up to the brim) or steam for 2 hours. Serves 4-6.

It is good served with LEMON SAUCE:
Boil 6 ozs. ($^3/_4$ cup) sugar with $^1/_8$ pint water for 5 minutes, then remove from the heat and add 2 teaspoons of butter and 1 tablespoon lemon juice. Stir until the butter is melted and pour over the top of the pudding.

Martin Matthews Esq., Helston.

Russian Cream

1 pint. milk
2 eggs
Sugar to taste
Gelatine, enough to set a pint of milk - ($1/2$ oz)

Put milk, sugar and egg yolks into a saucepan and place on low heat. Dissolve gelatine in 2 tablespoons of hot water. Add the gelatine to the mixture in the saucepan, raise the heat and continually stir until you see the milk just start to rise.

Turn off the cooker. Whisk egg whites until firm, add to the mixture quickly, stir and pour into a glass bowl, leave to set over night - not in the fridge. This will set in three layers - jelly base, mousse, and froth on top.

Customary in Helston on Flora Day and at Christmas

[Editor: Having received this recipe, I went home to make a Russian Cream and although it looked delicious, the taste was somewhat dubious! The result is pictured on the front cover.]

The Quarry List

Any bird you can shoot legally is termed a Sporting Bird. Within this definition are Game Birds (basically land birds) which come under the game legislation - and Wildfowl, which come under a separate Wildfowl Act.

The Birds Act of 1954 removed from the Quarry List many species formerly shot, such as Bustard. I have included here the species removed from the Quarry List since 1954 by the Wildfowl and Countryside Act of 1981. As from January 1994, all birds excepting those specifically undermentioned are protected by the Wildfowl and Countryside Act of 1981.

A Game Licence is required by any person shooting any bird or animal on the Game List and that includes Rabbit and Hare. No Game Licence is required for Wildfowl but owners' permission must always be obtained for shooting over private land. The Crown Estates are the legal owners of all foreshores between the high water mark and the land. Any person wildfowling requires permission either on an individual basis, or by automatic grant from the Crown Estates, (via The British Association for Sporting and Conservation - BASC), on becoming a member of the BASC, to carry firearms over Crown Estate Land where a right of way exists. Without such permission persons are liable to arrest for armed trespass. No gun is allowed to be carried in a public place unless it is secured against firing, is covered in a slip and has had its ammunition removed. Public place or private, the following oft quoted extract from 'The Art of Shooting' by Charles Lancaster, which was published in 1889, is well worth remembering:

> '*Never, never let your gun*
> *Pointed be at anyone,*
> *That it may unloaded be*
> *Matters not the least to me.*
> *You may kill or you may miss,*
> *But at all times think of this:*
> *All the pheasants ever bred*
> *Won't repay for one man dead.*'

Quarry and Shooting (Open) Seasons as at January 1994

~ Game ~

Grouse	Aug. 12th.-Dec. 10th.
Ptarmigan	Aug. 12th.-Dec 10th.
Blackgame	Aug. 20th.-Dec. 10th.
Grey Partridge	Sept. 1st.-Feb. 1st.
Red-legged Partridge	Sept. 1st.-Feb. 1st.
Pheasant	Oct. 1st.-Feb. 1st.
Capercaillie	Oct. 1st.-Jan. 31st.
Common Snipe	Aug. 12th.-Jan. 31st.
Woodcock	Oct. 1st.-Jan. 31st
Rabbit	No close season
Hares	No close season
	but may not be sold between March 1st. - July 31st.
Deer	See section below

~ Wildfowl ~

DUCKS:
- Mallard
- Teal
- Wigeon
- Pintail
- Shoveler
- Tufted Duck
- Gadwall
- Common Pochard
- Goldeneye

All duck & geese listed may be shot in and over High Water Mark of ordinary Spring Tides Sept. 1st-Feb. 20th. Elsewhere (i.e. inland) Sept. 1st.-Jan. 31st.

GEESE:
- Canada
- Greylag
- Pink-footed
- White-fronted
  (England & Wales only)

WADERS:

Golden Plover　　　　　　　Sept. 1st.-Jan. 31st.

VARIOUS:

Curlew	Common Scoter
Redshank	Velvet Scoter
Jack Snipe	Garganey
Bar-tailed Godwit	Goosander
Grey Plover	Bean Goose
Red-breasted Merganser	Stock Dove
Scaup	Rock Dove
Long-tailed Duck	

Moorhen	Sept. 1st.-Jan. 31st.
Coot	Sept. 1st.-Jan. 31st.
Pigeon (wood & feral)	No close season
Corvids	No close season

~ DEER ~

	ENGLAND & WALES	SCOTLAND
Red	Stags: Aug. 1st.-Apr. 30th. Hinds: Nov. 1st.-Feb. 28/9th.	Stags: July 1st.-Oct. 20th. Hinds: Oct. 21st.-Feb. 15th.
Fallow	Bucks: Aug. 1st.-Apr. 30th. Does: Nov. 1st.-Feb. 28/9th.	Bucks: Aug. 1st.-Apr. 30th. Does: Oct. 21st.-Feb. 15th.
Roe	Bucks: Apr. 1st.-Oct. 31st. Does: Nov. 1st.-Feb. 28/9th.	Bucks: Apr. 1st.-Oct. 20th. Does: Oct. 21st.-Mar. 31st.
Sika	Stags: Aug. 1st.-Apr. 30th. Hinds: Nov. 1st.-Feb 28/9th.	Stags: July 1st.-Oct. 20th. Hinds: Oct. 21st.-Feb. 15th.
Muntjac (Chinese Water)	No close season but British Deer Society recommend open season of Nov. 1st. - Feb. 28/29th.	As per England & Wales if appropriate

Species Removed from Quarry List
(by Wildlife & Countryside Act -1981)

Quail

The Common Quail (our native species) has been specially protected in the wild since before the 1954 Birds Act. The Japanese Quail, however, is available farm reared.

Swans

The Northern Ireland Wildlife Order of 1985 prohibited the shooting of Mute Swans in Northern Ireland. Prohibition in the rest of the United Kingdom was prior to this date. Bewick and Whooper Swans were given protection within the 1981 Wildlife and Countryside Act.

[I am indebted greatly to Miss. Stella Rees of The British Association for Shooting and Conservation at Marford Mill, Rosset, Wrexham, Clwyd for her help and information on this subject.]

The Parish Church of St. Mary, Truro ~ 1831.

The South Aisle, on the left of the print, is incorporated in the new Cathedral Church of the Blessed Virgin Mary, Truro and is called St. Mary's Aisle.

Hanging Game

Game should be hung in order for a certain amount of decomposition to take place. This tenderises the meat and brings out the flavour of the bird. Generally speaking - the older the game, the longer it should be hung. Hanging times given also depend upon the average temperature for the season. If the weather is warmer then normal, hang for the shortest time and if colder, hang for the longest. As a general rule, birds are ready for the pot when the breast feathers, inside leg and tail feathers can be easily plucked.

Game birds are hung by the neck, although it is rumoured that some foreigners hang them the other way up and I have tried it with pheasant to no disadvantage. There is an old theory that suggests one *should* hang a pheasant by the feet and when the body descends in a morbid heap to the floor, it is at just the right point of excellence! Hang in a cool, shady and well ventilated place which is preferably not in the dog kennel!

Nota Bene - when faced with a game larder burgeoning with rotting flesh, not a plucker in sight and the most disgusting smells are fast permeating the house and your partner is threatening to walk out - resist that feeling of rising panic, (which usually results in ignoring the problem for another day and becoming instead a woodchopper, a gardener or a motor car repair man). In fact do *not* begin to panic; instead systematically seize each bird in turn, apply a scalpel to its upper abdomen, make a slight incision through the skin, enough to accommodate a couple of digits of each hand and (gently) skin it! Pull the skin over the legs and around the wings which can all be snapped off at the upper joints. Next, yank the skin towards the beak and with a suitable hatchet, chop off its head. Next, gut and clean in the usual manner being careful to remove the crop. In your crazed and mazy daziness, resist the temptation of recycling for your howling infant's breakfast, that which you take to be sweetcorn!

This manic and frenzied activity may be accomplished in but a twinkling of the eye and is best achieved with a large and health-giving pink gin to hand.

APPROXIMATE HANGING TIMES FOR GAME

Blackcock	3-4 days.
Capercaillie	Hang until very tender or bury it in the ground. Exhume after a few days.
Grouse	2-10 days.
Hare	7-14 days - No more than 7 days without paunching. Paunch straight away if shot in the gut. Hang by back legs over a bowl to catch the blood. Make an incision between the muscle and the bone on one leg and feed the other leg through the hole to form a crook for supporting the hare on the hanging bracket. The blood must be saved for incorporation in the gravy for jugged hare. A teaspoon of vinegar in the bowl will stop the blood from congealing.
Partridge	2-10 days.
Pheasant	3-14 days. *[Ed: I have left them up to 15 days in fairly cold weather and they have tasted superb!]*
Pigeon	May be eaten fresh or left up to 3 days.
Ptarmigan	3-4 days.
Quail	May be eaten fresh or left up to 3 days.
Rabbit	Eat fresh and do not hang.

Snipe	These can be eaten fresh but may be hung up to 8 days. As these are often cooked with their entrails in place, do not leave too long.
Venison	3-14 days - The times depend very much on the animal. A young roe deer in prime condition may need only 3 days. A tough old fallow deer or red deer could require the full 2 weeks. Test each day of hanging by plunging a skewer into the haunch. This should not have an unpleasant smell when removed. If too high, wash meat in warm water and dry before cooking. Wrap the carcass in muslin before hanging in a a fly-free larder and keep muslin wiped dry of any moisture. If no larder, apply a generous quantity of mixed flour, pepper and powdered ginger. Be particularly careful to apply pepper to the furrow of the backbone.
Woodcock	These can be eaten fresh but may be hung up to 8 days. As these are often cooked with their entrails in place do not leave too long.
Woodpigeon	May be eaten fresh or left up to 3 days.
Wild Duck (Mallard, Teal, Wigeon etc.)	These may be eaten fresh or hung for a couple of days. Do not leave longer or the meat may become most unpleasant.
Wild Goose	1-2 days.

St Breock Partridge with Orange

Take two young Partridges and roast them lightly so that they are underdone. Pour off the juices and keep this hot. Melt an 'egg of Butter' *[Ed. - for this we suggest you visualise a hen rather than an emu or ostrich!]* Add a similar 'eggs' worth of Flour and one chopped Onion.

Cook for a few minutes. Add the juice from the birds, Meat Stock and a Bay Leaf, Thyme, half a teaspoon of made up Mustard, Salt and Pepper to taste, a splash of Sherry and a tablespoon of Cornish Clotted Cream.
Boil, then allow to simmer and reduce. Add the juice of half an Orange to the gravy. Cut the Partridges into two halves and lay them in the gravy in a suitable fireproof serving dish. Garnish with very thin strips of Orange Peel and toasted Breadcrumbs or Croutons.

Pheasant
(Roast and on Toast)

Place a tablespoon of Butter inside the bird, put into a roasting tin with another tablespoon of butter, melted, over the bird. Place in a hot oven and roast until tender - about an hour.
Meanwhile boil the Giblets (except the Liver) in about ¾ pint of water and a quarter of a pint of Wine Vinegar, add a Bayleaf; one Carrot; a small Shallot; a clove of Garlic; and Salt and Pepper. Simmer for 1¼ hours, then strain off the liquid. When the Pheasant is ready, remove from the roasting tin and keep hot.

Make a roux with a tablespoon of Flour and a tablespoon of Butter. Add the gravy from the roasting tin, the strained giblet liquid and a small teaspoon of Marmite and a teaspoon of Mustard. Add the chopped Liver, well squeezed through a fork and continue cooking for about 10-12 minutes, adding a little Port and Black Pepper to taste.

Cut pieces of Pheasant. Place on slices of Toast and pour some of the liquid over each.

This recipe is also good as follows:

To the original gravy, add: a few Button Mushrooms (perhaps a little Sweet-corn) and some small pieces of Red Pepper, before simmering the gravy liquid for the last 10 - 12 minutes. Place the cut roast Pheasant on to a dish and pour the gravy over it.

Serve with Breadcrumbs, fried in Butter, Bread Sauce and an Oatmeal Stuffing, (see under 'Stuffings').

JUGGED PIGEONS

4 Pigeons	Parsley
1 raw Egg	Fresh Butter
2 hard boiled Eggs	1 head of Celery
About 2 tablespoons Suet	Nutmeg
Flour	Sweet Herbs
About 2 tablespoons Brown Breadcrumbs	Mace
Pepper and Salt	4 Cloves
1 Lemon	White Wine - a glass

Pluck, draw and clean the birds and wipe dry inside and out. Boil the livers for a few minutes, then mince and mix with the yolks of the hard boiled eggs. Add the suet, breadcrumbs, grated lemon peel, sprig of chopped parsley, pepper, salt and a little nutmeg. Then mix in the lightly whipped raw egg and the softened butter. Divide mixture into four and stuff the birds, including the crops. Dip the birds in warm water, dredge with pepper and salt and put them into a jar with the chopped celery, sweet herbs, mace and white wine. Cover jar closely. Place jar in a pan of boiling water for 3 hours, topping up the water as necessary and keeping it gently boiling.

When birds are tender drain the gravy from the jar into a saucepan. Stir in a knob of butter well rolled into some flour. Cook until thick and quite smooth. Pour over the pigeons, serve and garnish with slices of lemon.

PARTRIDGE STEW

Brace of Partridge
Dripping for frying
One or two slices of Ham
1 Tomato
6 Button Mushrooms

1 clove of Garlic
6 Peppercorns
4 Cloves
Stock and a little salt
Glass of Port Wine

Cut up the birds into joints and fry lightly to brown a little. Put them in a stew pan or casserole with the ham, cut into pieces. Add the rest of the ingredients. Pour over a glass of port with stock sufficient to cover all. In a stew-pan, simmer slowly for two hours. If cooking in a casserole, place in hot oven, then lower heat after 10 minutes and continue in slow/medium oven for the rest of the time.

CORNISH HEN PHEASANT
(WITH CREAM CHEESE OR COTTAGE CHEESE AND APPLE)

(Particularly useful for frozen and/or skinned birds, as this process tenderises them)

Many fine pheasant shoots in Cornwall produce an abundance of birds in the season. The quickest way to deal with a surfeit, is to skin them and then freeze them (which saves the bother of plucking); or to freeze them complete with feathers after hanging (but without innards) and then skin them when they begin to thaw. At this stage they skin particularly easily.

Wipe dry the inside of the bird and then stuff with about 2 tablespoons of Cream Cheese or Cottage Cheese and one cooking apple (peeled, cored and chopped). Wrap the bird in streaky bacon rashers and then in cooking foil. Roast in a moderately hot oven for 45 -50 minutes (or until done). Unwrap the bird, carefully preserving all the juices which are then thickened with cornflour if preferred, or served as unadulterated gravy.

I usually serve skinned birds sliced and jointed with a watercress garnish.

[Editor: This is a delicious recipe and the cheese and apple stuffing is excellent with cold pheasant. I have served the above with an additional 'Light Oatmeal Stuffing' - see under 'Stuffings'.]

Mrs P. Copeland, Trevilla, Nr Truro.

RABBETS TO CHUSE

A female rabbet is much better to eat y^n a buck rabbet; now a female rabbet hath a little bitt of whitish skin on each side with ye belly just below ye kidneys, but a buck hath not.

Then an old rabbet hath a little knob on ye first joint of ye two fore feet wch a young rabbet hath not.

Besides an old rabbet is easily known from a young one when skinn'd by ye colour of ye flesh.

[Taken from Receipts of the 17th. and 18th. Century within the family papers of Pendarves of Pendarves, Camborne. C.R.O. No. PD 324.]

TERRINE OF PHEASANT

2 Brace of Pheasant
1 lb. Belly Pork
$^3/_4$ lb. Streaky Bacon Rashers
$^1/_2$ lb. Pig's Liver
2-3 Wineglasses of Madeira
1-2 Wineglasses of Brandy
2 chopped Onions
3-4 tablespoons Clotted Cream
3 tablespoons Tomato Chutney*
6 ozs. field Mushrooms
Zest, juice and pulp of 1 Orange
Aspic Powder

1 teaspoon dry Mustard powder
1$^1/_2$ teaspoons of ground Ginger
1 teaspoon Cinnamon
$^1/_2$ teaspoon of Nutmeg
1 teaspoon All Spice
1 teaspoon Tandoori Spice Blend
Black Pepper - lots, to taste
Salt - to taste
1 teaspoon Garlic Powder
1$^1/_2$ teaspoons of Mixed Herbs
Juniper Berries

*See Binkies Tomato and Apple Chutney recipe within this book.

1. Skin, dress and pressure cook pheasants at 15 lbs. for 30 - 40 mins.
2. Take the meat off the bones, (leaving the breast meat intact) and place in bowl.
3. Dice belly pork into $1/2$" squares and gently fry until cooked and some of the fat has rendered down.
4. Lightly fry the streaky bacon and dice the majority into small pieces, leaving a few whole rashers for garnishing.
5. Place all meat in the bowl and marinade in the Madeira and brandy, spices and herbs, overnight.
6. Lightly fry onions and field mushrooms.
7. Mince all the meat (except the breast meat), with the onions and mushrooms.
8. Carve the breast meat into slices.
9. Make sauce up to nearly one pint with more Madeira and brandy and add the aspic powder.
10. In the terrine, place a layer of breast meat slices and pour over a little of the sauce. Continue by adding a layer of minced game followed by further breast meat and diced bacon. Add more sauce. Continue in this manner until the terrine is full.
11. On the top layer, place some whole bacon rashers and Juniper berries and glaze with further sauce.
12. Cook in a slow oven for about half an hour.

K. F A.

Then home through the hot, sweet-smelling Summer lanes,
Gay with the first foxgloves and purple vetches,
Red sorrel and golden crowsfoot in the hedges,
To Sunday dinner, family round the table
Together, who now are all scattered, east and west,
And one has gone to his eternal rest.

A. L. Rowse.

At both harvest and threshing the farmer provided lunch at his table for all his workers and these meals were treated as something of an occasion. This was the scene one summer's day in about 1908 at Trewey Farm, St. Levan.
William Trewern sits at the head of his table.

The Silver Swan

from
The First set of Madrigals and Motets of Five Parts (1612)
by Orlando Gibbons (1583 - 1625)

The Silver Swan, who, living, had no note,
When death approached unlocked her silent throat;
Leaning her breast against the reedy shore,
Thus sung her first and last, and sung no more:
Farewell all joys, O death, come close mine eyes;
More geese than swans now live, more fools than wise.

Swan - The Bird Royal

'*Farewell all joys, O death, come close mine eyes; More Geese than swans now live, more fools than wise!*' The joy of the swan is now, more than ever before, in the eye of the beholder - but this was certainly not always the case. Swan was a favourite food for kings and the rich in the earlier centuries of this millennium and most certainly graced the banqueting tables of the aristocracy and gentry of Cornwall on feast days such as Christmas and upon other especial occasions. Indeed we are told by Winston Graham in 'Ross Poldark' the third of the Poldark novels, that swan was served at Trenwith for Christmas Dinner in 1787! A tenuous substantiation, I agree, but based very definitely upon fact.

Fact and fiction are intrinsically linked to the history of the Bird Royal. As in the poignant works of the Orlando Gibbons poem; does the swan sing her first and last as death approaches? Is this the origin of the 'swansong'? And is the freshwater swan seen gliding in baronial lakes the same species as the bird of the sea shore and saltwater creeks? Is it true that Her Majesty The Queen owns all swans? Is swan still eaten today and if so how is it prepared? As I started to delve into this fascinating subject, I realised that my knowledge of the swan was was extremely limited. I hope the next few pages provide some interesting answers to those questions and others.

There are three varieties of swan as resident in and visitor to Britain. The Mute Swan or Cygnus Olor is the large bird resident in Britain and well known for its spotless white plumage, black legs and orange-red bill surmounted by a black knob which is larger in the male than the female and known as the 'berry'. It builds its nest upon a great mass of aquatic plants sometimes piled to a height of up to two feet and sometimes extending to a diameter of six feet in which it lays between five and nine greyish-olive eggs. The young hatch after a five to six week incubation period and are covered in a sooty-grey down followed by feathers of the same colour. It can be up to a year before the cygnets lose all their immature feathers and take on the familiar snow white appearance of their parents. Up to

200 years ago it was noticed that certain cygnets on the River Trent were born white and they and their parents had legs of a paler colour. They were given the name of Cygnus Immutablis and became known as the 'Polish' swan. They are now regarded as but a variety and have no connection with Poland.

The Whooper or Whistling Swan (Cygnus Musicus) in the main is a winter visitor to Britain from Iceland, save for a tiny breeding population in Scotland which stay all the year round. The Whooper Swan is of nearly the same size as the Mute Swan and is of equally white plumage. Its carriage is totally different but just as graceful as that of the Mute Swan and it is recognisable by its lemon-yellow and black tipped bill. The musical tones it utters have been celebrated from ancient times. Of close relation to this bird is the much smaller Bewick Swan (Cygnus Bewicki) which breeds in the high arctic of Russia and only winters here. It makes a tuneful cry but does not have the melodious sounds of the Whooper. The Mute Swan is, as I have said, here all the year round. It makes odd noises from time to time but is not a very vocal bird and hence its name. Swans create their sounds by the passage of air travelling through the trachea and I am told by The Queen's Swan Warden that it is *possible* that a dying swan *could* make a noise as its last passage of air leaves the body, but there seems to be a certain scepticism with regard to this ancient and oft referred to legend; the Swansong. The Oxford English Dictionary tells us that 'swansong' has its origin in the German Schwanensang or Schwanengesang and states 'A song like that, fabled to be sung by a dying swan.' Orlando Gibbons (in the poem at the beginning of this article) has the origin of the legend very definitely linked to the Mute Swan. 'The Silver Swan, whose living had no note, When death approached unlocked her silent throat.' Franz Schubert wrote a cycle of seven songs to unrequited love entitled 'Swanengesang' and further on the subject of singing, Samuel Taylor Coleridge is a stern critic of one poor singer whom he sums up succinctly by saying: 'Swans sing before they die - 'twere no bad thing, did certain persons die before they sing.' As a professional concert singer and teacher, I do, at times, sympathise with him completely! If any readers can enlighten me further in the matter of the swansong, I should be delighted to hear from them.

Swans prefer fresh water and do not do as well in salt water and they tend not to breed in salt water if it can be avoided. This is probably because they seek a richer supply of aquatic vegetation in order to rear the cygnets. They will always drink fresh water by preference, although it is probable that they have a filtration system against salt.

And now to ownership. It is recorded that between 1247 to 1251, Henry II issued a series of requisitions for provision to the Sheriffs of different Counties adjacent to those places where he happened to be going to keep the chief feasts of the year. In 1247, the provision for Christmas at Winchester included forty swans. In 1249, two requisitions were made for a total of 104 swans. The Royal status of the swan was being put to the test as early as the 15th century when it was known that 'certain persons having the charge of swans had stolen cygnets and hence yeoman and husbandmen and persons of little reputation became possessed of swans.'

'Thus it was' and I quote from a leaflet most kindly supplied by the Clerk of the Worshipful Company of Dyers 'that in 1483 an Act of Parliament was passed (22 Edw. IV C.6) which enacted that no other than the King's sons could possess a 'game' of swans or a swan-mark unless the individual received a grant from the Crown and was possessed of freehold land or property to the annual rental value of 5 Marks. This gift of the Crown granting the privilege of a Game of Swans and a swan-mark was a freehold of inheritance and could be handed down to one's heirs. A condition of the gift was that every bird in a 'game' should bear a distinguishing mark of ownership on the bill.' This is termed the cygninota.

The Abbot of Abbotsbury in Dorsetshire enjoyed such a privilege and had such a Game in the estuary formed by the Island of Portland and the Chesil Bank and after the Dissolution of the Monasteries, the privilege was granted to the ancestors of the Earl of Ilchester. The City of Oxford too, had a Game of Swans by prescription and in the 16th. Century no state dinner was complete unless swan was included in the fare.

A great many private individuals as well as Institutions and Corporations owned swan-marks through the 16th and 17th centuries. The marks were nearly always on the upper mandible and mostly of complicated design, some even incorporating elements of the arms of the owners.' There is, extant, a full register of the marks of Elizabethan times when the ownership was probably at its highest, standing at something over 900 swan-marks which were recognised by the Royal Swanherd, whose jurisdiction extended over the whole Kingdom.

Swan keeping was often the source of great revenue to the owner, whose rearing costs were practically nothing. The Dyers' Company publication continues 'In 1274 the price of a swan as food was fixed by the 'Statua Poletrice' of the City of London at three shillings, whereas the best capon could be sold at $2^{1}/_{2}$d., a goose for 5d. and a pheasant at 4d. Before the advent of the turkey, swan was customarily eaten at Christmas and no banquet was complete without them.

The City of Norwich maintains a Swan Pit which originally was used for the fattening of swans and cygnets for the table and at one time Norwich swans were gastronomically almost as famous as Norfolk turkeys.'

The Worshipful Company of Dyers and the Worshipful Company of Vintners both hold Royal Charters granting them the right to hold a 'Royalty of a Game of Swans' on the River Thames. Neither Company has an exact record of the respective date of grant, but it is thought that the Vintners' acquired the privilege in 1483 and the Dyers' in about 1550.

I am most grateful to a source who wishes to remain anonymous for much valuable and fascinating information upon the 'Royal Bird' and with reference to the legal right of the Crown to own the swan, I quote from our correspondence:

> *'The most recent affirmation of this right is to be found in the "Wild Creatures and Forest Law Act of 1970." In practice, the Crown only lays claim (or The Queen only exercises the prerogative right in the ownership of swans) to the swans on the River Thames from Dorchester downstream as far as Sunbury (and its tributaries and some adjacent waters). Strictly speaking, this ownership is restricted to the Mute Swan (Cygnus Olor).'*

Each year on the Monday of the third week in July there is held upon the River Thames, the ceremony of Swan Upping. I quote from the 'Royal Encyclopædia': 'The Royal Swan Marker, accompanied by a representative of the Lord Chamberlain's office, The Queen's Swan Uppers and the Swan Marker of the Vintners' Company and the Swan Master of the Dyers' Company and their men set off upstream from Blackfriars in six rowing boats known as Thames skiffs. The journey up river usually lasts for five days and covers the stretch of the Thames from Sunbury to Pangbourne. Each day they seek out all the broods of cygnets and their parents along the river. The first man to sight a brood shouts 'All up!' - the traditional call warning all the boats to get into position to catch the swans. When the birds are caught, the marks on the parent swans' beaks are examined to establish their ownership (swans without marks belong to The Queen, those with a mark on the right of the beak to the Dyers' Company and those with a mark on each side of the beak to the Vintners' Company) and the cygnets' beaks are then marked in the same way. As they pass Windsor Castle, they stand to attention in their boats with oars raised to salute 'Her Majesty The Queen, Seigneur of the Swans'.

Special uniforms are worn for swan upping. The Royal Swan Marker wears a scarlet jacket with brass buttons, white trousers and a peaked cap with a white badge of the Royal Crown. On his left arm is another badge depicting a swan encircled with the words 'HER MAJESTY'S SWAN MARKER'. The Queen's Swan Uppers are dressed in scarlet jackets and white duck trousers. The Vintners' Swan Marker wears a green coat with silver braid and buttons and has a peaked cap with a white cover and white trousers. The badge on his cap and jacket is of the Company's arms. The Swan Master of the Dyers' Company has a blue coat with gold braid and brass buttons, white trousers and a peaked cap with a white cover. His badges also bear the arms of his Company. The Vintners' men wear white jerseys and white trousers, while the Dyers' men are dressed in blue jerseys and white trousers.

The Thames skiffs bear special flags for the occasion. The Queen's boats have a white flag depicting the Royal Crown and the Royal Cypher. The Vintners' flags show a swan on a red background with the Company's badge in one corner and the Dyers' have a blue flag with a swan and the Dyers' badge in one corner.'

Swan Upping is far from being only a ceremonial event. It provides a useful opportunity to monitor breeding figures, analyse general health, weight and size of cygnets, or check for injuries caused by fishing line and hooks et cetera. During the 1970's the number of Swan deaths, particularly on the Thames, was increasing at such an alarming rate that extinction was becoming a real possibility. A three year scientific survey was commissioned to find that the primary cause of death was from lead poisoning from lead fishing weights. The sale of lead fishing weights was banned eventually in 1987, since when the population has maintained a steady growth - although the problems are far from over, which is why the careful monitoring continues.

It is right to record that both the Dyers' and Vintners' Companies treasure and value their Royalty and both expend money for the care and attention for the birds within their ownership. Wild swans receive none of this attention and have to take their chances along with all the other wild birds, save for the protection afforded them under the Wildfowl and Countryside Act of 1981.

Each year the Dyers' and Vintners' Companies hold the traditional Swan Dinner and Swan Feast respectively. It must be stressed that no longer are any birds killed specifically to eat and the swan served is meat from birds which have died within the year from natural causes or accident. This is then frozen until the annual banquets. The Dyers' Company serve Dyers' Cygnet, which is a dish often mixed with goose and sometimes they serve a swan sausage. I am most grateful to the Chef to the Vintners' Company who has supplied their recipe, which is printed within this volume.

Swans were also maintained at Cambridge University and in 1433-4 they are first mentioned in the records of The King's Hall, which was the forerunner of Trinity College. It is known that The King's Hall maintained eight swans in 1437-8 and in 1451-2 is the first reference to a Swanherd. Alan Cobben in 'The King's Hall' informs us that after the later date 'the accounts contain copious entries for the capture, inspection and marking of the swans.' 'Swans were also bought for immediate consumption and these are listed separately in the section for stores. It seems, too, that a number of swans were maintained privately as there are entries in the accounts for the purchases of swans and for their foodstuffs by Warden Richard Caudray and three of the Fellows in 1439-8.' Certainly swan was traditionally served each year at the May Ball at St. John's College, Cambridge and this ancient custom continued until 1986. Other colleges at Cambridge also had rights of ownership.

I end this article by recounting a sad and sorry tale of a young schoolboy, far away from home and wandering one day in the flood meadows of the River Nene at Oundle in Northamptonshire. Suddenly, that small boy came upon a dead swan, still warm, which he bore back to his housemaster[*] (first mistake - moral - don't be so gullible!), in triumph (second mistake - moral - pride before a fall!). The housemaster, whom I shall generously not name, appropriated it as his own (third mistake - don't forget the old adage 'I see it, I like it, it's mine!'), and held a very grand dinner party, after which he informed the small boy how delicious had been his 'gift'. The small boy (who is now forty years old), tasted not a morsel of the Bird Royal. He remembers however, the words of fellow Old Oundelian,

[*]Not P.O.C.E.

sometime housemaster, wit, broadcaster and raconteur, the well known Arthur Marshall, who puts it succinctly in his marvellous autobiography 'Life's Rich Pageant': 'Never imagine that children don't notice and remember *everything*' he goes on 'Our old chum, the poet Burns, had a phrase for it - 'A chield's amang you taking notes'!' *He was!* Moral - to end as I began,- (and I don't know which bit is the more appropriate to the small boy or to the housemaster) *'More geese than swans now live, More fools than wise'!*

Swan

Peter Gladwin, Executive Chef to the Worshipful Company of Vintners, to whom we offer our thanks for this information and recipe writes:

"Swan was traditionally served as a centre piece for a feast. The bird would be plucked, trussed and roasted, then covered with a cured skin and feathers like a 'tea-cosy' to resemble an upright live swan. Nowadays a stuffed swan is still ceremonially presented, but the cygnet meat is used to make a more appealing dish served as one of the courses of the meal."

In olden times, the bird would sometimes be served with its wing feathers replaced after roasting and it would be borne into the room with a piece of blazing camphor - giving off an aromatic smell, or a lighted wick in its mouth, which must have been a spectacular sight in a candlelit dining room. At the Vintners' Swan Feast, it is announced as "cygnet for your delectation." Cygnet is served in preference to swan, being much more tender. It is not hung for any length of time and is generally cooked within 3-4 days.

CYGNET

With: (i) Wild Mushroom (ii) Sage Sauce (iii) Cranberries and Orange

Roast the cygnet upon a wire rack (in the same manner as for a goose) for between 2½-3 hours. A substantial amount of fat drains from the bird during cooking. Allow the bird to go cold and then take the meat off the bone. Boil the carcass with the giblets. With a small quantity of the fat, make a brown roux sauce by adding the stock. Now add a good quantity of lightly fried wild mushrooms and the juice. Add sherry and sherry vinegar, a little mustard, brown sugar, and seasonings to taste. Place meat upon a serving salver and pour over the sauce. Decorate with pastry ornaments cut in the shape of a swan.

This recipe may also be varied by the use of sage instead of mushrooms within the sauce or by adding cranberries and orange. In the later case, additionally garnish with long thin strands of very finely pared orange skins, which have previously been gently steamed until tender (but not over cooked, as the colour must be preserved).

CYGNET WITH CHAUDRON
(TRADITIONAL RECIPE)

After roasting the cygnet it was traditionally accompanied by Chaudron. This is a broth made from the birds' own intestines and blood, with the addition of vinegar and strong spices - perhaps not so widely used today!

N.B. Shakespeare used the word 'Chaudron' in 'The Witches Scene' from 'Macbeth'.

St. Just-in-Roseland

'This is the place where the boats are moored'

Saint Just in Roseland

Ecclesia Sancti Justi-de-Lansioch-in-Rose

This is the place where the dead are moored
to everlasting buoys beside the boats.
The Creek is everywhere. The Church floats
like a seabird whose neck is the tower.
Flight of the heron to Turnaware.
    Bird country, boat country . . .

This is the place where the boats are moored
beside the churchyard, in green canvas dressed.
The dead sleep feet pointing East.
The seagull cries, voice wet and windy.
Growth - vegetation - stillness - beauty -
    Sea country, water country . . .

The Church is the Ark. I am Noah.
Here, I would save the seabirds first. The Hill
leans back, dark green, wide open, never full,
although for centuries, layer on layer,
Cornishman, foreigner are laid here.
    Cormorant country, curlew country . . .

Patterns of lines assail me: the vertical
as the line of life: masts, trees, I
still vertical, perpendicular. Boats lie
like bodies of the dead: horizontal:
correct posture for sailing off to eternal
    time country, God country . . .

Zofia Ilinska.

Seakale in Parmesan

(This is thought to be Mary Dingle's recipe of c.1860.)

Cut the Seakale in about 3" lengths. Boil for 15-20 minutes. Pour over it ½ pint of Parmesan Sauce. Sprinkle with grated Parmesan and serve hot.

[Editor: Her Parmesan Sauce recipe is missing! We suggest a basic white sauce to which add Parmesan cheese, a little grated strong cheddar and seasonings to taste which could include a little mustard.]

Tomatoes au Gratin

(This is thought to be Mary Dingle's recipe of c.1860.)

Cut off the tops, scoop out the seeds without breaking the outer skin. Put them in a stew pan with 2 ozs. Butter. Chop finely some Button Mushrooms, some Parsley, 4 or 5 Chives or some pieces of Onion, some chopped Ham and fat Bacon, fry all together for 5 minutes and add the yolk of 2 eggs. Fill the tomatoes up with the mixture and sprinkle some breadcrumbs over them, putting a small piece of butter on each. Let them fry quickly 10 minutes and serve.

Leek & Potato Pie

Into a buttered oven dish, slice some Leeks thinly and season lightly with Salt, Pepper and Mixed Herbs. On top of this, slice thinly some Potatoes and season likewise. Continue with alternate layers, with the top layer of potatoes placed neatly round the dish, each lapping slightly over the other until full. Pour 2-3 tablespoons of Milk round the top edges of the dish. Dot the top with Butter and drizzle over the whole a teaspoon or two of Clotted Cream. Place the dish in a moderate oven for about ¾ hour until well cooked and lightly browned on top . According to the oven temperature the dish can be covered at first, taking it off to brown for the last 5-10 minutes. Delicious with cold meats.

M. F A.

Swedes with Bacon

Place in a saucepan thin slices of Smoked Bacon with a layer of sliced Swede on top. Repeat these layers alternately until you have the quantity you need. Add 2 tablespoons cold water, place on low heat to simmer gently until cooked. Delicious.

Pat's Cornish Farmhouse Carrots

2 Carrots	Mixed Herbs
2 Leeks	Mustard
2 Onions	Seasoning
White Sauce	Clotted Cream

Chop carrots and leeks and gently boil in salted water, giving the carrots a few more minutes than the leeks. Chop onions and lightly fry in a deep skillet in butter. To the fried onion, add butter and a couple of wooden spoonfuls of flour and mix well. Add milk to make sauce. Add a generous quantity of mixed herbs and a good teaspoon of ready mixed mustard. Drain the leeks and carrots and add to mixture. Grind black pepper over the vegetables and add a tablespoon of clotted cream. (White wine may be added if desired.)

Very tasty with cold meats and baked potatoes.

Mrs. Brooke.

Stuffings

Versatile Oatmeal

1 Forcemeat Stuffing for Roasts:
4 heaped tablespoons Pinhead Oatmeal (Coarse)
¼ lb. Suet
1 Onion, chopped
Salt, Pepper and Herbs to taste
2 Tablespoons Sultanas
Little chopped Apple

Mix all ingredients together well. Add a little hot water and stir to stuffing consistency. Leave about 10 minutes to cool, then use as desired.

2 Light Oatmeal Stuffing - (or as a side dish for savouries):
4 tablespoons Pinhead Oatmeal
2 tablespoons medium Oatmeal
3 ozs. Butter, cut in pieces
Salt
2 teaspoons ground Ginger
1 teaspoon Marjoram

Mix all ingredients except the butter. Add a little boiling water to soften. Stir all together and leave for a while until cold, when the oatmeal will have swollen a little. If necessary then add further boiling water to loosen the mixture. Place in a fireproof dish and dot with small knobs of butter. Cook in a moderate oven until nicely browned.

[Recommended with Cornish Hen Pheasant recipe.]

3 As a savoury topping for fish or meat pies:
Use the ingredients as in **2** Mix all ingredients except the butter. Then rub the butter into the dry ingredients. Cover the pie with this, as for a crumble.

4 As a sweet fruit crumble:
4 ozs. Pinhead Oatmeal
2 ozs. Medium Oatmeal

4 ozs. Butter
2 tablespoons Brown Sugar
A little cinnamon or other flavouring if desired.

Rub the butter into the rest of the mixture and spread over the fruit of your choice. Bake in moderate oven till browned.

M. F A.

DIPPIE

Boil potatoes and pilchards in thin cream or dippie. This dish is called "Dippie" and was very popular before cream was demanded by the factories.

Penzance W.I.

[Taken from 'Cornish Recipes - Ancient and Modern', edited by Edith Martin and originally published by the C.F.W.I. in 1929.]

FORCEMEAT BALLS

2 rashers of lean Bacon (or Ham)
2 Eggs - beaten
¼ lb. Suet
3 ozs. Breadcrumbs
3 ozs. Medium Oatmeal
2 teaspoons of finely chopped Mixed Herbs
1 teaspoon of Parsley
Rind of half a Lemon
Cayenne Pepper
Ground Mace (about a saltspoon)
Salt   } To taste
Pepper
(Adjust all quantities to your requirements)

Mince finely the bacon rashers and the lemon rind. Mix together and add the breadcrumbs, oatmeal, suet, herbs, spices and seasonings and moisten with hot water. Add beaten eggs and incorporate the whole. Dampen with a little more hot water, if required. Form into balls and fry in dripping until brown or bake in a moderate oven for about half an hour. Do not overcook as they should be moist when cut through. Excellent with Jugged Hare, Turkey and Chicken.

Creamed Chestnut and Brandy Stuffing

---

10 ozs. cooked Chestnuts
3 dessertspoons Clotted Cream
1 pinch of Basil to taste
Ground Black Pepper
A little Salt

1 oz. melted Butter
2 dessertspoons Brandy
2 teaspoons Lemon Juice

} To taste

Boil chestnuts until soft, skin and chop finely into a fireproof bowl. Add all other ingredients and bake gently in a moderate oven.

For stuffing fish, the ingredients need to be blended into the consistency of paste and spread over one half of the cut fish and then parcelled up on greased greaseproof paper before baking.

This stuffing is very good with mackerel.
Sufficient for 4-6 persons or for stuffing 4 medium sized fish.

K. F A.

Stuffings for Meats

(a) Base -

    4 to 5 tablespoons Pinhead Oatmeal (coarse)
    4 ozs. Shredded Suet
    1 Onion, chopped
    Salt, Pepper.

(b) Added ingredients of your choice:

    1-2 handfuls of Sultanas
    1 chopped Apple or other fruit
    Some Celery, chopped
    A few chopped Nuts

(c) Mixed Herbs - including:
    Sage
    Marjoram   *One or more*
    Mace   *according to your*
    Parsley   *taste with the meat.*
    Thyme

(d) Fruit Juices - for example:
    Orange Juice
    Lemon Juice

Mix base ingredients well, add herbs of your choice for the meat and then add some of the other ingredients as desired. Finally mix all together with a little hot water to melt the suet and soften the oatmeal. Let it stand for 10 minutes and stuff the meat.

SUGGESTIONS:

With Chicken:
    Sultanas and Celery
    Mixed Herbs - including Marjoram
    A little Lemon Juice

With Duck:
    Sultanas
    Mixed Herbs
    The fruit of half an Orange, chopped
        (or Orange Juice)

With Pork:
    Sultanas
    Chopped Apple
    Mixed Herbs including Sage

Many people add an egg to stuffing. I prefer it without - but experiment. The art of cooking is to smell and taste your herbs etc., and choose those ingredients you think will complement the meat. You may be delighted with the result, to much approval!

Note: If you have no coarse oatmeal, porridge oats are a good substitute.
M. F A.

How many miles to Mylor?

How many miles to Mylor
  By frost and candle-light:
How long before I arrive there,
  This mild December night?

As I mounted the hill to Mylor
  Through the dark woods of Carclew,
A clock struck the three-quarters,
  And suddenly a cock crew.

At the cross-roads on the hill-top
  The snow lay on the ground,
In the quick air and the stillness,
  No movement and no sound.

'How is it?' said a voice from the bushes
  Beneath the rowan-tree;
'Who is it?' my mouth re-echoed,
  My heart went out of me.

I cannot tell what strangeness
  There lay around Carclew:
Nor whatever stirred in the hedges
  When an owl replied 'Who-whoo?'

A lamp in a lone cottage,
  A face in a window-frame,
Above the snow a wicket:
  A house without a name.

How many miles to Mylor
  This dark December night:
And shall I ever arrive there
  By frost or candle-light?

A. L. Rowse.

DRINK AND THAT 'ONE FOR THE ROAD'?

A CAUTIONARY TALE OF SIMON THE CELLARER, COZ - HIS WIFE AND POOR LITTLE BESSIE.

(Ramblings thorough Quotations)

Now Simon was a pleasant child, fair of face, easily pleased, and with a bright and happy future before him. But it has to be said that although he had a prodigious memory for quotations, he was slightly naive when young and rather easily led by the suggestions of others. His was a God fearing family who oft quoted the Bible and he remembered that within a certain parable the ground of a rich man brought forth plenteously and he also remembered that the rich man addressed himself saying 'and I say to my soul, Soul, thou has much goods laid up for many years: take thine ease, eat, drink and be merry!' As he grew out of childhood and into youth he considered this an excellent maxim and conveniently forgot the rest of the parable. He also remembered that the Old Testament suggests that 'a man has no better thing under the sun, than to eat and to drink and to be merry!' He particularly enjoyed that last two thirds of the quotation and began to consider it his daily duty. He had read Hamlet and was encouraged by Shakespeare's 'one for the road' policy: 'We'll teach you to drink deep, ere you depart' and upon departing he had often set himself the task of walking the white line, but always he had failed. He was not a bit downcast for he loved his country and remembered 'before the Roman came to Rye or out to Severn strode, The rolling English drunkard made the rolling English road' (G.K. Chesterton) Yes - you have guessed correctly, I tell this sad tale of an Englishman, for this could never happen in Cornwall. Indeed it has a second cautionary warning for the Cornishman, who shall surely heed this story and make it his business never to leave these hallowed shores.

I return to Simon for whom youth and charm were synonymous and in those spring days (when partaking of the tipsy cake) his thoughts would often be directed towards the daughter of the landlord of his local hostelry, who was a comely serving maid. He would stare into her liquid eyes and say "drink to me only with thine eyes And I will pledge with mine" (Johnson). If I might interject with an interpolation, or in other words interjaculate, it has to be said, most sadly, that in later life he became less polite and rather vulgar. Creating a problem for the poor girl's oculist he would slur in a loud and crude voice "Ere's mud in yer eye" - but I digress. Besotted by those eyes which drank to him only, the handsome and by now not quite so naive Simon, begged of his comely friend for a song to melt the heart; well we all know the old adage 'if music be the food of love', and it did - he was butter in her hands. We also know 'How silver-sweet sound lovers' tongues by night. Like softest music to attending ears' (Shakespeare). She filled his flagon to the brim and he quoted "O Coz, Coz, Coz (for that was her name), my pretty little Coz, that thou didst know how many fathom deep I am in love" (Shakespeare - again 'with you' is implied). Buoyed up by the silvern hop he continued:

> ' "You elegant fowl, How charmingly sweet you sing!
> Oh let us be married! Too long we have tarried;
> But what shall we do for a ring?" '
>
> Easily solved when you know the right person:
>
> ' "Dear Pig, are you willing to sell for one shilling
>   Your ring?"
> Said the Piggy "I will"
> So they took it away and were married next day
> By the turkey who lives on the hill." '

Well he'd got her and soon after the death of her father he'd got the tenancy of the pub too.

Soon; O how very soon, the road to ruin was paved with no good intentions. But we all know that life has to continue and after the appointed gestation it did. Horace told us as long ago as 65 B.C. that 'Mountains will heave in childbirth and a silly little mouse will be born,' save that he told us in Latin, which sounds much more poetic - 'Parturient montes, nascetur ridiculus mus.' Her name was Bessie. Things deteriorated and the regulars would sing the old song by W.H. Bellamy which was appropriate to Simon's ideas of moderation for a healthy physique:

> 'Old Simon the Cellarer keeps a large store,
> Of Malmsey and Malvoisie
> And Cyprus, and who can say how many more!
> For a clever old soul is he
> Of Sack and Canary he never doth fail
> And all the year round there is brewing of ale
> Yet he never aileth, he quaintly doth say
> While he keeps to his sober six flagons a day.
> > But ho! ho! ho! his nose doth show
> > How oft the black Jack to his lips doth go.'

Well this became too much by far for poor Coz to bear. She remembered, slightly inaccurately, the words of a former prime minister and one heady day she girded up her loins and screamed:

"Simon you are drunk, Simon you are very drunk, Simon you are very drunk indeed".

It must be said that this came as something of a shock to Simon who, quick as a flash, rejoined with:

"Madam you are ugly, Madam you are very ugly, Madam you are very ugly indeed - but I shall be sober in the morning!"

Coz was distraught - and took to the gin. It is now quite widely known as 'Mothers' ruin' and indeed for poor dear Coz it was. She was very soon 'gathered and rejoiced with them but upon another shore'. In later years George Bernard Shaw by way of an explanation used to say to little Bessie 'Gin was Mother's milk.'

As you can imagine, with no fair maid to warm his hearth, Simon was in the 'Slough of Despond'. He applied unto himself that which almost amounted to an intravenous drip of neat alcohol, in the mistaken belief that oblivion was the best course ahead. Of course he became a derelict ruin and lost everything. His landlord took the pub in hand and threw poor Simon and dear little Bessie out into the dark and stormy night. (We must remember that this all occurred before the days of the omnipotent Social Services Department). The final scene in this tragic tale is best recounted by the Victorian wordsmith 'Stella' (whomever she might have been), who overheard poor Bessie's poignant words:

>'Out in the gloomy night, sadly I roam,
>   I have no mother dear, no pleasant home;
>Nobody cares for me - no one would cry
>   Even if poor little Bessie should die.
>Barefoot and tired, I've wandered all day
>   Asking for work but - I'm too small they say;
>On the damp ground I must now lay my head -
>'Father's a Drunkard and Mother is dead!'
>Mother Oh! Why did you leave me alone
>With no one to love me, no friends and no home?
>Dark is the night, and the storm rages wild,
>God pity Bessie, the Drunkard's lone child!'

These words were set to music, becoming a very popular Victorian ballad and had they not largely been forgotten, A.A. would have stood (today) for none other than the the Automobile Association - which is, of course, the only 'one for the road!'.

∞

Mahogany

(Sometimes called Black Strap - because of its colour)

Take 2 parts gin to 1 part of Treacle and beat the mixture together.

This was a great favourite with the fishermen who loved this drink due to its warming properties. Thomas Bond in his 'History of Looe' in 1823 refers to a story which occurred at one of the Cornish Assizes, the gist of which is as follows:

'It was enquired of a witness as to his specific occupation at a given time and place. The judge and learned counsel were somewhat amazed to hear that the witness had been 'eating fair maids' (cured pilchards) and drinking 'Mahogany'!'

Kea Damson Gin

Kea Damsons are well known in Cornwall and can form the basis of the most delicious liqueur. Three quarters fill a 7 lb. stone marmalade jar with previously frozen (or pricked) Damsons. Cover with White Sugar and stir daily, closely covering the jar after each time you have had a stir.

Again, a couple of spots of Almond Essence may be added after filtering - as for Sloe Gin. Damson Gin is a more subtle flavour than Sloe Gin and the two may be combined half and half for yet another delightful liqueur.

Sloe Gin

Gather sloes (the fruit of the blackthorn) in September or October and place in freezer until required. The old method required one to prick each sloe several times with a silver bodkin which was definitely a job I used to hand over to my Grandmother and it kept her out of mischief for a good many hours!

As she approached and passed the age of 100, it seemed unfair to expect her to work so hard for her supper (not that sloe gin was ever her usual supper, I hasten to add!) and I discovered that by freezing the sloes the same effect was created.

Three quarters fill a $1^1/_2$ pint jar (which must have a screw top lid) with de-frosted sloes and cover generously with soft brown sugar. Agitate daily for some weeks or months until all the juice is removed from the sloes which turn pulpy. When required, or when one has a spare bottle and a half of gin, place sloes in a 7lb. stone marmalade jar (or suitable crock) and add the gin. Stir, cover and repeat stirring daily for a few days, then strain through muslin several times. Add 2 or 3 spots of almond essence to taste - which makes all the difference.

The pulp of sloes precipitates a considerable sediment and to obtain crystal clear sloe gin, it is necessary to filter the liquor through a wine maker's filter pad. If this is not done, the sloe gin may form further sediments at a later date - if it lasts that long!

Sloes used also be served in a pie known as 'Sloney Pie" and this caused the good people of St. Dennis much trouble. Their pie was so ill appreciated that one is told the mention of sloes to a St. Dennis man became a heinous insult!

Homemade Lemonade (called Citric Acid)

1lb. Sugar
3 - 4 teaspoons Citric Acid
2 Lemons
1 pint Water

Place sugar in a large jug. Add citric acid and the juice from the lemons. Pour on boiling water and place the lemon halves in the jug. The recipe can be varied by the substitution of other citrus fruits.

Cider

Long ago, Cider was as widely drunk in Cornwall as it is to this day in Devonshire. Every farm had its own cider press and we are informed by Mr. Hamilton Jenkin in 'Cornwall and its People' that according to Mr. Bath in his 'Uncle Kit's Legacy' a 'Siah Penpol, was one of those old fashioned people who always put a toad into the cask of cider and by that means the refreshing drink seemed to be purified by passing again and again through the creature's body. Indeed no cider was considered to be up to the mark unless it had a toad to "work" it'. Mr. Hamilton Jenkin remarks that this extraordinary practice appears to have been the norm and it is believed that toads sometimes lived for over twenty years in this fermenting work. He explains further that 'when the cask was empty, the creature would be tipped out through the bung hole and the people standing by would exclaim ' "Mind the toad, mind the toad, save 'un up for the next brewen"!'

Shenagrum, Schnagram, Shenackerum or Schnack

This was a great favourite for drinking at Christmas. There are various alternatives depending upon region but the most common is as follows:

Boil $1/2$ a pint of home-brewed Beer and add:
$1/2$ a noggin* of pure Jamaica Rum,
Soft Brown Sugar to taste,
a Sliced Lemon,
Grated Nutmeg to taste.

Mr. Morton Nance, writing in the Western Morning News on 23rd. February, 1929 tells us that:

'It (Shenagrum) appears to have derived its name from the familiar dog-Latin expression of 'super naculum' meaning 'on the nail'.'
'In the Sixteenth Century', he continues, 'when the phrase first appeared in England, it was used in connection with a custom of reversing the glass and letting its last remaining drop fall on the thumbnail, whence it was licked to show that the liqueur was not shirked. A little later we find it used of any drink so excellent and rare that no drop of it should be wasted and, still later, an adjective 'supernacular' was coined to describe such a drink.'

[*A noggin is the same measure as a gill - both equalling a quarter of a pint.]

GINGER BEER

To one ounce of Best Powdered Ginger, 2 ounces of Cream of Tartar and one Pound of Loaf Sugar - pour one Gallon of <u>Boiling</u> Water. Cover it and let it stand for 12 hours then add 2 tablespoons of yeast. Let it stand 12 hours more - then strain and bottle for use.
  N.B. It should be made in an open vessel.   (This recipe is dated c.1820.)

(Taken from a Kennel and Game Register from the records of the family of Gulley Bennet of Tresillian House, Newlyn East. Held by the C.R.O.)

ELDERFLOWER SYRUP

1½ lbs. Granulated Sugar   1 Grapefruit
2 pints boiling Water   1oz. Citric acid
2 small Lemons   6 large Elderflower heads

Mix sugar in a large bowl with boiling water. Add zest of lemons and grapefruit. When cool add the juice of the fruits, citric acid and elderflowers. Cover and stand overnight. Strain over a bottle. Store in the fridge for up to 1 month.

Mrs. Michael Stone,
Trevince.

HERBY BEER OR BOTANIC BEER

Caramel	Acetic Acid
Locust Bean gum	Liquid Capsicum
Extract of Horehound	Oil of Lemon
Extract of Quassia	Oil of Nutmeg
Extract of Quillaia	Oil of Rosemary
Extract of Dandelion	Oil of Cassia
Extract of Yarrow	Oil of Cloves
Extract of Comfrey	Oil of Hops
Extract of Nettle	Oil of Thyme
Extract of Burdock	Oil of Lime
Oleo Resin Ginger	

Take 2 tablespoons of extract of all the above ingredients and add to this 1-1½ lbs. of sugar. Pour over 1 gallon of boiling water. When cold, add a further 1 gallon of cold water and 2 tablespoons of barm, or 1 oz. of yeast. Let it stand in a warm place for 6 - 12 hours. Pour off the clear liquor and bottle using good corks.

"This Preparation makes an excellent Beverage giving flavour, colour and heavy Herb-like bottled ale."

[Editor: This recipe comes from a farmer's wife in Camborne. It was drunk by her family at harvest time some fifty years ago. Stone pitchers were carried out into the fields for a mid-day refreshment.]

METHEGLIN
(Dated 1698)

Metheglin proceeds from the Improvement of Bees and thus it is made, viz., after the Honey is drained from the Combs as much as may be, they steep them in a small Wort made of Malt and Water and press out the remaining sweet through a Bag, the Wort being cold, then they add several handfuls of Rie Meal and a pint of new Milk to each Gallon, being first curdled posset-wise and the Curd taken off them; adding more Honey, they boil up the Wort and so draw it off into Casks, where, being settled and well purged, it is drawn off into Bottles and kept for use, being very cool and pleasant. Penzance.

[Taken from 'Cornish Recipes - Ancient and Modern', edited by Edith Martin and originally published by the C.F.W.I. in 1929.]

Messrs T. Rowe, 83, Lemon Street, Truro ~ 1900.

A Cornish Oven

A CLOME OB'N AND A "BAKER"

"You ask me to write and tell you what a "clome ob'n" is like. Well, I will do my best.

I take it that you never saw one. That is a pity, for I dunno which will be the hardest, to describe it or to imagine if from the description. You must know that years and years ago, before Watts, his name, invented steam, or coal mines were discovered, that people still ate bread, at least, perhaps not so much as they do to-day. I believe they used to eat more oatmeal and more "fry teddies;" still what bread there was had to be baked somehow, and I believe the first and oldest way of baking bread or anything else, was by means of a "flat ire" in the open chimbley.

I have baked on it scores of times before we had one of the new fashioned "apparatusus," and my mother never baked on nothing else, except in the "clome ob'n." We only heated the latter for a big baking, say once a week or so.

The "flat ire" was "etted up" quicker, and was plenty big enough for a few pasties or a roast, or tart, or anything we might want for dinner or tay.

We first of all put the "flat ire" on the brandis (a three-legged iron affair) and then we lit a fire under it of sticks and "brimbles," furze and anything that would give a clear "ett," and after about twenty minutes or so the the "ire" would be white 'ot, and the fire would be allowed to die down, when we would take out the brandis, and "drop the ire," (a round heavy sheet of iron with a handle at each side) among the ashes, wiped off whatever ashes was on it, and drop our loaf of bread, or whatever we were going to bake, right in the centre. The "baker" (it looked like a huge iron frying pan without a handle) was then turned over on it and red-hot ashes piled up all over and that was all there was to do.

If it was a loaf of bread it took about an hour, and lovely bread it would be, too.

Now I will try to tell 'ee how to "Ett a Clome Ob'n."

The oven (or ob'n) is simply a hole in the wall of the chimbley, there must be hundreds of them walled up in Cornwall, for every old house had one, and I daresay some have still got them.

They are oval in shape and are roofed over with a hard white substance which gave it the name of "clome". It took about an hour to "ett," and the fire had to be kept burning clear all the time the fire was in it of course and at first it would all turn black, but gradually it would grow white.

Blackthorn was the favourite fuel for heating it with, and the ashes had to be kept raked out, so the bottom would get hot as well as the sides and roof. When it was white 'ot to the very door, the ashes were thoroughly cleaned out and the tins of bread and plum cake put in (our oven would hold ten tins), the door was shut and red ashes piled around it to keep out any draught, and there you were, nothing more to do till it was ready to come out an hour later, a lot less trouble and a whole lot cleaner than blackleading a new fashioned apparatus to my mind."

ST. KEA W.I.

(The above was given in response to an appeal for a description of the old ways of baking bread, cakes, pasties and such like, by a member of the Cornwall Federation of Women's Institutes living at St. Kea and originally published within the volume 'Cornish Recipes - Ancient and Modern', compiled by Edith Martin and published by the C.F.W.I. in 1929.)

BAKING IRON AND KETTLE

Heat baking iron to red heat. Heat kettle. Place bread or cake on iron, cover with kettle, surround with hot cinders and cover with burning furze and turf. Bake 1 to 1^1/$_2$ hours according to size.

ST. JUST W.I.

(The above was taken from 'Cornish Recipes - Ancient and Modern', published by the C.F.W.I. and compiled by Edith Martin.)

1. Salter
2. Pitcher
3. Bread pancheon or cloam
4. Croust box
5. Pitcher
6. Salter (bath shaped) for pilchards or mackerel
7. Lemon squeezer
8. Colander
9. Bussa
10. Wash hand basin (with built in soap dish)
11. Salter
12. Spice box
13. Chyl or chylla

1. Racking hook
2. Meat jack
3. Cloam oven
4. Fire crooks (to lift off baker to see if food was cooked)
5. Salt box
6. Crock
7. Brandis
8. Urn
9. Cloam oven
10. Scrowling grid
11. Jam kettle
12. Baker
13. Baker
14. Ire

Cornish Range

In regular use at the house of Mr. and Mrs. Eric Berry. This Cornish Range was made in Redruth by the manufacturers, Messrs. Terrill and Rogers and dates from the late 19th. Century.

Sauces

In Victoria's reign, during the Edwardian years and up to the First World War, the French were of the opinion that the English kitchen contained three taps - one for hot water, one for cold and one for White Sauce.

Marquis Domenico Caracciolo (1715-1789) wrote (in French):
'In England there are sixty different regions, - and only one sauce.'

When all these recipes fail, do not despair for Miguel De Cervantes, (1547-1616) has the answer:

'Hunger is the best sauce in the world!'

[Editor: I have observed this to be true - as we tend to dine rather late, we have often noted with amusement that if we starve our guests long enough, they fall to with a will, eat anything placed before them and make not the smallest hint of complaint.]

Spiced Gooseberry Sauce

- 1 pint of Gooseberries
- 1 dessertspoon Sugar (more sugar if fresh gooseberries)
- 8 dessertspoons of Gooseberry Syrup (if using tinned gooseberries)
- 1 heaped tablespoon: Clotted Cream
- $1/4$ teaspoon Basil
- $1/2$ teaspoon Ground Ginger
- $1/2$ teaspoon Ground Nutmeg
- 1 heaped tablespoon: 1oz. Butter

Gently cook the gooseberries with the sugar and sugar syrup. Add all other ingredients and adjust flavour to taste. This sauce may be thickened if desired by adding a little cornflower mixed with a small quantity of water. *Excellent for Goose and Mackerel.*

Spiced Gooseberry and Stilton Sauce

Make gooseberry sauce to the above recipe and crumble into pan between $1^{1}/_{2}$-2 ozs. of ripe Stilton to taste. (Probably more will be required if the cheese is not mature).

A good accompaniment to Gammon or Steak.

Horseradish Sauce

5 tablespoons of freshly grated Horseradish
1 1/2 teaspoons of Caster Sugar
Black Pepper and Salt to taste
2-3 teaspoonfuls of ready made Mustard
Clotted Cream
Wine or Cider Vinegar

Mix together the sugar, freshly grated horseradish and seasoning. Dampen with a little vinegar and add about 4 dessertspoons of clotted cream. If this is required to be served hot with fish heat gently in a bain marie and watch very carefully to make sure it does not boil, lest it should curdle. *Serve cold with Beef.*

Mustard and Clove Sauce

Make a usual white roux sauce with plenty of butter and add a generous teaspoonful of previously made Mustard (to taste) and a good handful (approximately 20) of Cloves. Simmer to extract the flavour of the spice. *This makes an excellent accompaniment to Roast Gammon or Smoked Gammon.*

Lemon and Cream Sauce (for Salmon)

(Sufficient for 4-5 persons.)

6-7 ozs. Unsalted Butter
Thyme
Double Cream

Juice of 1 Lemon
Salt and Pepper to taste

Heat the butter fairly slowly to frothing then add the juice of lemon, stirring all the time with a whisk. Add fresh thyme, finely chopped, and the salt and pepper to taste. Bubble away for 3-4 minutes. Add the cream IMMEDIATELY before serving (1 dessertspoonful - 1 tablespoonful). Whisk vigorously and continuously until serving after the addition of the cream.

Mr. Marc Gregory, Truro.

Asparagus Sauce

5 Spears Asparagus
2 ozs. Butter
1 Wineglass of White Wine

$1/2$ lb. Clotted Cream
Salt
White Pepper

Chop asparagus finely and sauté very gently in butter to soften. Blend, leaving out some of the tips which are added back at the end. Return to pan and add white wine. Boil furiously to reduce a little. Take off heat and stir in the clotted cream. Add seasonings and the asparagus tips. Serve when warmed through.

Caramel Sauce

Melt an ounce of soft Butter and add 2 or 3 tablespoons of Brown Sugar. When bubbling, add Cream and Sherry - stirring all the time.
This makes a delicious sauce to pour over bananas or ice-cream.

Green Tomato Mincemeat

(This is an excellent way to utilize the last green tomatoes of the season)

5 lbs. Green Tomatoes
2 lbs. Brown Sugar
1 lb. Raisins
1 lb. Currants
$1/2$ lb. Mixed Peel
$1/2$ cup Vinegar - (8 tablespoons)

$1/2$ cup Butter (4 ozs.)
1 teaspoon each of ground:
Cinnamon
Cloves
Nutmeg
Mace

Chop tomatoes finely and drain. Bring to boil and simmer for 30 minutes. Add everything except the spices. Stir well and boil until thick, which will take about 2 hours. Do not overboil. When cold, add the spices. Keep in glass jars and seal with wax.

Penhalvean.

[Editor: I am grateful to the lady who gave me this invaluable recipe and who lived at Penhalvean. Her name eludes me and should she like to contact the Tredinnick Press, we shall be happy to offer her a gratis copy of this book.]

BINKIE'S TOMATO AND APPLE CHUTNEY

6 lbs. Ripe Tomatoes (quartered)
3 lbs. Cooking Apples (minced)
1½ lbs. Preserving Sugar
¾ oz. Salt
(2 ozs. in 1½ times the quantity)

1 pint Malt Vinegar
2 large Onions (minced)
½ cup cold Water
1½ good teaspoons ground Ginger
Black Pepper

Boil the tomatoes in cold water for 1 hour. Remove all the skins by straining through a sieve and add everything else. Boil for another 3 to 4 hours. This chutney is fairly runny and is part way between chutney and sauce.

> N.B. If this is too sweet, it may be sharpened up by the addition of a little lemon juice.

Mrs. (Binkie) Wallen, Hayle.

MRS. (KATIE) BOLITHO'S WINDFALL JELLY

(Taken from the handwritten Victorian recipe book)

"All sound apples which fall, no matter how small were collected until I had four or five pounds. They were shaken in a cloth to remove dirt and dust, put into a preserving jar, well covered with water and placed over a low gas where they remained with the addition of a dozen cloves, until they began to burst and the flavour of the fruit was distinct in the liquor. As this process is carried out very gently no watching is required, all that is necessary is to see that they do not go to a pulp. When the skins were broken, but the fruit still whole, I strained the liquor off through a hair sieve and left it to cool so that any sediment might sink to the bottom. Next I weighed the liquor and adding one pound of sugar and the juice and rind of a lemon for each pound of liquor. I put the whole to boil over a high gas. When it came to the boil I let it gallop for half an hour, stirring well. I then took out the lemon rind and potted the liquor which, now of a deep orange colour, jellied almost immediately. It has been greatly appreciated by all who has tasted it."

Penzance.

Pickled Apples

(Taken from Mrs. Bolitho's handwritten Victorian recipe book)

5 lbs. Apples
1 lb. Sugar (brown)
1 pint Vinegar

3 Cloves
A little Whole Spice

Boil the sugar; vinegar; cloves and whole spice. Then add the apples.

Penzance.

No Alcohol Mincemeat
(November 1919)

1 lb. Suet
1 lb. Apples
1 lb. Sugar
1 lb. Raisins
1 lb. Currants

2 ozs. Peel
1 oz. Sweet Almonds
2 spoons Spices mixed
2 Lemons

Mince all the fruit and then thoroughly mix with the suet; sugar and spice. Press into a clean dry jar and tie down.

[This is taken from Grandma Hutchens's recipe book. Her Grandson, Mr. Lester Bolitho, informed us that as a strict Methodist, she never touched alcohol.]

Penzance.

Salad Dressing (Delicious!)

(Taken from Mrs. Bolitho's handwritten Victorian recipe book)

2 Eggs
$1/2$ oz. Mustard
$1/2$ pint Milk

$1/2$ oz. Salt
$1/4$ lb. Caster Sugar
$1/2$ pint Vinegar

Break egg into basin but do not beat it. Work in salt; mustard; sugar; milk and lastly the vinegar, all consecutively. Place in a saucepan and simmer or boil slowly until a thin cream. Keep stirring all the time.

Sunset at Towanroath Shaft, Wheal Coates, Chapel Porth.

Bibliography

(consulted in research for the articles herewithin contained.)

'Cornish Cookery' by Vida Heard, published by Truran, 1984.

'Cornish Recipes - Ancient and Modern', edited by Edith Martin, published by the Cornwall Federation of Womens Institutes, 1929.

'Cornwall and its People' by A.K. Hamilton Jenkin, published 1945 and re-published by David and Charles (Publishers) Ltd., 1970.

Encyclopædia Britannica, Eleventh Edition, 1910-1911.

'Father's a Drunkard and Mother is Dead' by 'Stella', from the 'Parlour Song Book', edited by Michael Turner and Anthony Miall and first published by Michael Joseph Ltd., 1972.

'Hawker of Morwenstow - Portrait of a Victorian Eccentric' by Piers Brendon published by Jonathan Cape, London, 1975.

'Life's Rich Pageant, the Autobiography of Arthur Marshall', published by Hamish Hamilton Ltd., 1984.

'Macbeth' by Shakespeare, taken from 'The Windsor Shakespeare', edited by Henry Hudson, published by The Caxton Publishing Company, London.

The Oxford Dictionary of Quotations, published by Oxford University Press.

'Ross Poldark' by Winston Graham, published by Fontana Books, 1969.

Royal Encyclopædia.

'Simon the Cellarer' by W.H. Bellamy from 'Just a Song at Twilight', edited by Michael Turner and Anthony Miall, published by Michael Joseph Ltd., 1975.

The King James Bible, printed by Charles Bill and the Executrix of Thomas Newcomb deceased, Printers to The Queen's most Excellent Majesty, 1706.

'The Helston Furry Dance' (Official Booklet), published by The Flora Day Association, 1989.

The King's Hall, by Alan Cobben.

'The Silver Swan', by Orlando Gibbons, from 'The First Set of Madrigals and Motets of Five Parts', published in 1612.

'The Sporting Wife, Game and Fish Cooking', edited by Barbara Hargreaves published by H.F. and G. Witherby Ltd., London, 1979.

'The Art of Shooting' by Charles Lancaster, originally published in 1889.

'Tour Through Cornwall' by the Revd. Mr. Warren.

'Victorian and Edwardian Cornwall from Old Photographs' by John Betjeman and A.L. Rowse, published by B.T. Batsford Ltd., London, 1974.

'Wheal Jane - A Clear Way Forward', published by the South West Region of the National Rivers Authority.

ACKNOWLEDGEMENTS

The Editor and Publishers are greatly indebted to the many persons and institutions listed here below, who have given most generously and unstintingly of their time and expertise and without whose help this little book would not have been possible. It is our sincere hope that this list is complete. We have been truly amazed by the quantity and quality of the enthusiastic help we have received and we offer to all, our humble thanks.

ARTICLES AND GENERAL RESEARCH

Anon; The Staff of the Cornish Studies Library, Redruth; The County Archivist and the Staff of the Cornwall County Record Office; Martin Matthews Esq., Curator of the Helston Folk Museum and Kerrier District Council; The Worshipful Company of Dyers; The Worshipful Company of Vintners; Miss Quarmby, Assistant Librarian, St. John's College, Cambridge; Jonathan Swift Esq., The Library of Trinity College, Cambridge; Miss Stella Rees,The British Association for Sporting and Conservation; The Very Revd. David Shearlock, Dean of Truro; The Revd. Canon Robin Osborne; Duncan Simpson Esq., W.R. Nicholas Ltd., Chemists, Redruth; Tony Brown Esq.; Devonshire Record Office; Dr. Noel Kantaris; Miss Angela Broome, Librarian, The Royal Institution of Cornwall; Ministry of Agriculture,Fisheries and Food; Mrs. Colin Hyde; Dr. Randolph White; West Country Studies Library, Exeter; Michael Martyn Esq.; Mr. and Mrs. Nicholas St. Aubyn.

RECIPES

Miscellaneous Anonymous Donors; Mrs. Fraser Annand; Mrs. (Binkie) Wallen; Mrs. Brooke; Mrs Lester Bolitho; Miss Lynne Hirst; Peter Gladwyn Esq., Executive Chef to the Worshipful Company of Vintners'; Mrs. Michael Stone; Mrs. Nicholas St. Aubyn; Mrs. P. Copeland;
Mrs. Peter Wilkinson alias Lily Champney; Mrs. Thomson; Marc Gregory Esq.; Tredinnick Family; Martin Matthews Esq; Mrs. Webber; Miss Wendy Eathorne; Mrs. Hill; Mrs. Swiss; Mr. and Mrs. Alex. Keir; Mrs. Grey; C.R.O. and families of Pendarves of Pendarves; Rashleigh of Menabilly and Richard Gully Bennet Esq., late of Tresilian House, Newlyn East. (Gulley Bennet records deposited by Messrs. Whitfield, Solicitors, St. Columb Major.)

POETRY

'Ruan Lanihorne' and 'Saint Just in Roseland' are reproduced here by kind permission of the poet, Zofia Ilinska and are taken from her collection of poems entitled 'Horoscope of the Moon', which is published by Tabb House of Padstow.

'How Many Miles to Mylor'; 'Westcountry Folksong; Child's Verses for Winter' and an extracted verse from 'The Old Cemetery at St. Austell' are reproduced here by kind permission of the poet, Dr. A.L.Rowse and are taken from his collection of poems entitled 'A Life - Collected Poems - A.L. Rowse' which is published by Messrs. William Blackwood of Edinburgh.

Marjorie Fraser Annand, for her educational poem with regard to methods of cookery employed on Shrove Tuesday, entitled 'Pancake Day'.

PHOTOGRAPHS

The Royal Institution of Cornwall; *(8, 10, 15, 22, 47, 53, 111)*; F.E. Gibson Esq.*(65)*; Graham Hill Esq.*(5)*; Reg. Watkiss Esq.*(83)*; Tredinnick Press Photographic Library *(1, 21, 37, 56, 69, 84, 88, 94, 102, 114, 115, 121, 124).*

MISCELLANEOUS

Mrs. Fraser Annand (proofreading, miscellaneous services and general encouragement); Michael Stone Esq. (proofreading); Kerry Taylor (typing, typesetting and solving in an uncomplaining fashion, all those problems with the computer created by the Editor and the Designer); Miss Rebecca Hyde (for use of her computer); Robin Davidson Esq.; Peter Riches Esq.; Ferrers Vyvyan Esq.; Roger Penhallurick Esq. - The Royal Institution of Cornwall; C.R.O. and families of Tremayne and Francis Buller Howell Esq. (for publishing information taken from their family records); Mr. and Mrs. Stephen Kingwell (advice on fish).

INDEX

SOUPS & SAVOURIES:
Chonion Tart 6
Cornish Vegetable Soup 7
Dame Nellie's Pate 6
Parsnip & Asparagus 4
Sarah's Mushroom Savoury 4
Stilton Soup (Gwennap) 7
Treviskey Soup 3

FISH:
Cockles 17
Fish Pie 20
Fish Pie (Comford) 20
Gurnard 16
Limpets 16
Lobster - to roast 18
Mackerel 16
Mussels 17
Oysters 18
Pilchards 17
Salmon Cutlets 16
Salting Pilchards 16
Smoked Mackerel Custard 19
Sprats - to pickle 19
Trout Pye 19

MEAT:
Beef - Christmas Spiced 30
Brawn - Chicken & Pork 27
Chicken Galantine 28
Cornish Sausage 25
Gammon & Apricot Pie 31
Gerty Meat Pudding 33
Hare - Jugged 26
Kidneys (Alehouse) 31
Lan'cen Pie 32
Market Day Special 27
Pasty - Genuine! 28
Pork - Tenderloin fillet in
   Mead & Cider Sauce 29
Pork - Sweet Pickled 30
Steak - Jugged 30
Steak & Kidney Pudding 32
Turkey (Penponds House) 25

GAME:
Partridge Stew 80
Partridge (St. Breock) with Orange 78
Pheasant (Cornish Hen)
   with Cheese & Apple 80
Pheasant - Roast & on Toast 78
Pheasant - Terrine of 81
Pigeons - Jugged 79
Rabbits - to Chuse 81
Rabbit - jellied 26
Swan - roast 92
   Cygnet with
   (1) Mushrooms (2) Sage Sauce
   (3) Cranberries & Orange 93
   Cygnet with Chaudron 93

STUFFINGS:
Creamed Chestnut with Brandy 100
Dippie 99
Forcemeat Balls 99
Stuffings for Meats 100
Versatile Oatmeal 98

SAUCES:
Asparagus 118
Caramel 118
Gooseberry - Spiced 116
Gooseberry - Spiced with Stilton 116
Horseradish 117
Lemon & Cream 117
Mustard & Clove 117
Salad Dressing 120

VEGETABLES:
Cornish Farmhouse Carrots 97
Leek & Potato Pie 96
Seakale in Parmesan 96
Swedes with Bacon 97
Tomatoes au Gratin 96

PUDDINGS:
Bread & Butter 61
Celtic Delight 64
Chocolate Marquaise 60
Christmas Pudding
   (Grandma Hutchens's) 61
Figgy Hobbin 59
Floury Milk 59
Gerty Grey 59
Gerty Milk 60
Helston Pudding 68
Lemon Curd Sponge Pudding 58
Pancakes Supreme 62
Plum Pudding (St. Breock) 56
Russian Cream 69
Victorian Imperial Pudding 58

CLOTTED CREAM:
To Make 56

BAKING:
Apple-Hot (Auntie Ethel's) 45
Black Cake (Tredinnick) 43
Bread & Bread Rolls 48
Chocolate Grenades 52
Christmas Rum Cake
   (Gt.Gt. Aunt Eliza's) 42
Cider Cake (Pat's) 45
Cornish Boiled Cake 50
Cornish Heavy Cake 50
Cornish Lemon Drizzle 49
Great Cake 51
Hazelnut Gateau (Mother's) 46
Mock Almond Tartlets 44
Penzance Cake 51
Raspberry Puffs 49
Saffron Cake (Mrs.Penhaligon's) 42

Spiced Buns 49
Violet Cake 44

CHUTNEY & PRESERVES:
Apples - Pickled 120
Mincemeat Green Tomato 118
Mincemeat-No Alcohol 120
Tomato & Apple Chutney 119
Windfall Jelly(Mrs.Bolitho) 119

BEVERAGES:
Cider - Ancient method of
   Fermenting with Toad 108
Elderflower Syrup 109
Gin - Kea Damson 106
Gin - Sloe 107
Ginger Beer 109
Herby Beer 110
Lemonade - homemade 108
Mahogany 106
Metheglin 110
Shenagrum 108

ARTICLES:
A Cornish Oven 117
Drink - and that
   'One for the Road' 103
Fish, Foods, Famines and Fables 8
Hanging Game 75
Helston Flora 66
Puddings, Cakes and Biscuits 54
Swan - The Bird Royal 85
The Quarry List 70
The Story of Saffron 38

POETRY:
How Many Miles to Mylor 102
Pancake Day 63
Ruan Lanihorne 36
Soup 2
St. Just in Roseland 95
The Silver Swan 84
West Country Folksong 21

MISCELLANEOUS:
Assize Court Menus (1911) 34
Lent Assizes (1605) 23
Tredinnick of St. Breock 57

To be Published in Time for Christmas, 1994.

Remedies and Reminiscences

The Second Book in the Series
'A Taste of Cornwall'

A taste of which is on the next page! This book will contain 17th. Century to early 20th. Century Remedies (herbal and otherwise); Interviews and Articles about different aspects of life in Cornwall and photographs of the County, some ancient and some especially taken for this book. If you have enjoyed 'Recipes and Ramblings', we hope that you will order your copy of 'Remedies and Reminiscences' through your bookshop in Cornwall or alternatively if you live out of the County, directly from us. If you order from us, please send a cheque made out to Tredinnick Press in the sum of £7.50* plus £2.50* (to cover postage and packing) to Tredinnick Press, at Burnwithian House, St.Day, Cornwall, TR16 5LG.

*Prices hold until 31st. December 1995.

Caveat Lector

The Editor with stern advice,
Advises, lest you pay the price
That all these treats and potions fare
Are mingled not with God's clean air;
And this dire warning thou shalt heed
Lest some poor soul wears widows weed
So should you suffer maladies
DO NOT ATTEMPT THESE REMEDIES,
For if you fall to deep malaise,
Or suffer death, or go part craze,
And with malodorous intent
Then think to sue and are hell bent,
I shall refer you to this lay -
Thou shalt not prosper 'pon that day,
For hid within these words so wise
Are warning capitals to prize;
And this disclaimer shall be deemed
By all mankind from friend to fiend,
To cover, joint and several,
Wherein, at law, is usual
The libraries and book seller
The publishers and editor.

Kenneth Fraser Annand,
Tredinnick Press.

℞ = Take

A Water to Wash ye Face

℞ of gascoign wine 2 q^r.ts. put it 8 of flax food bruised. 6 pippins pared and sliced, 2 lemons sliced, 4oz of rosemary flowers, balm, one handful raisons stoned, & bitter almonds blanch'd and beaten, ½lb: a quart of fatt snailes, a couple of fatt puppy dogs of 8 or 9 daies old, flay & gutt them & wipe them clean, but not wash yem; cutt them in little peices, so putt all into your still & still it wth a gentle fire.

[Taken from 17th. and 18th. Century Receipts within the papers of Pendarves of Pendarves, Camborne. C.R.O. No. PD 324.]

A Farting Powder

Cos. Wightwicke's

℞ yellow skin at ye bottom of a gooses foot, dry it in an oven & powd^r it & give ye party some of it, & in an hours time it will work briskly. Probat.

[Taken from 17th. and 18th. Century Receipts within the papers of Pendarves of Pendarves, Camborne. C.R.O. No. PD 324.]

Hair to make Grow

Edwd. Luttrell

℞ 3 live frogs, burn them in a pott & take ye ashes & mix with yem a little honey or tarr, yen rub ye place y^t is bare, and you will see ye affects.

[Taken from 17th. and 18th. Century Receipts within the papers of Pendarves of Pendarves, Camborne. C.R.O. No. PD 324.]

To Drive and Keep your House Free from Rats and Mice

One ounce of Assasalid, one ounze of Tincture of Myrh, 2 ounces of Venice Turpentine, one ounce of Burgundy pitch, 3 drachms of oil of Swallows, pound these all together make it into a small Pill as big as a pea, put them into holes or on the walls or 5 or 6 under the Bark floor or other place and all the Rats will depart in 24 hours, to be done once a year.

[Taken from the Rashleigh Papers. C.R.O. No. R5681.]

Re-drawn from a 17th Century Map.

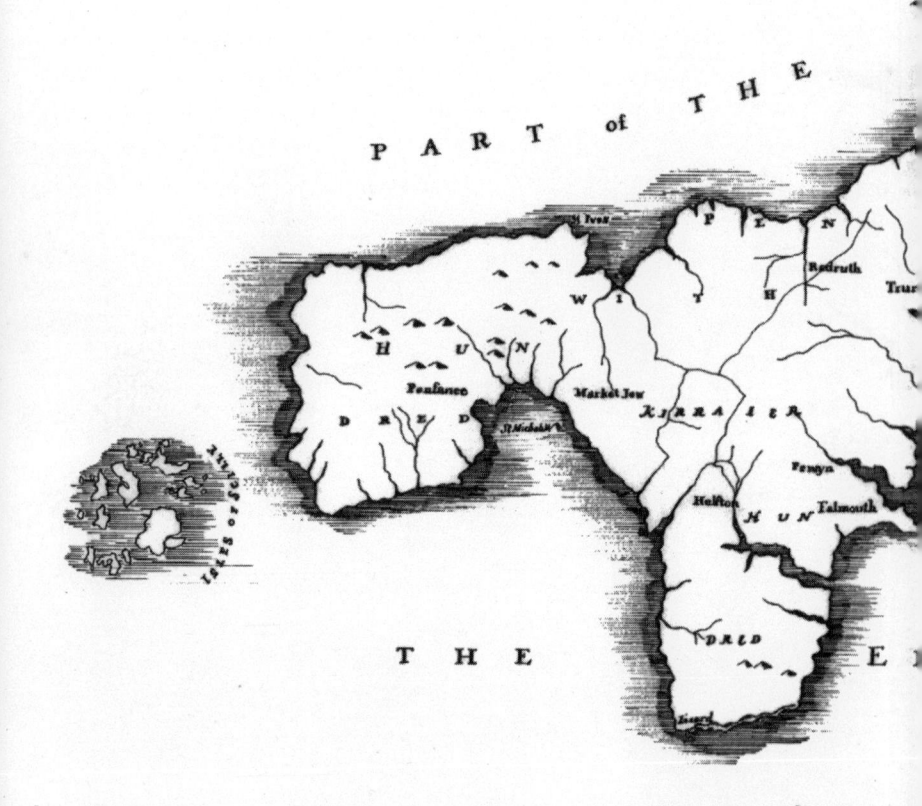